FOLK ART WEATHER VANES

Authentic American Patterns for Wood and Metal

John A. Nelson

Stackpole Books

Published by
STACKPOLE BOOKS
5067 Ritter Road
Mechanicsburg, PA 17055

Printed in the United States of America

First Edition

10 9 8 7 6

Library of Congress Cataloging-in-Publication Data
Nelson, John A.
    Folk art weather vanes : authentic American patterns for wood and
metal / John A. Nelson.—1st ed.
        p.   cm.
    ISBN 0-8117-2406-9
    1. Woodwork. 2. Metal-work. 3. Weather vanes—United States.
I. Title.
TT200.N36   1990
736′.4—dc20   89-26368
                                                                                    CIP

Folk Art Weather Vanes

CONTENTS

ACKNOWLEDGMENTS

The following people helped me obtain information and photographs: Marie A. Turley, Assistant Commissioner of the City of Boston; Phil Bergen, Librarian, The Bostonian Society; William E. Worthington, Jr., Museum Specialist, National Museum of American History; Paula Locklair, Director, Old Salem, Inc.; Joan P. Whitlow, Curatorial Assistant, Essex Institute; Alberta M. Brandt, Photographic Supervisor, Winterthur Museum; Kate Jones, Manager, The Old South Meeting House; Carl R. Salmons, Chief of Museum Services, Saugus Iron Works; Penelope H. Batcheler, Historian, Independence National Historical Park; Karen L. Otis, Photographic Services, Museum of Fine Arts, Boston; Albert O. Louer, Director, Media Relations, Colonial Williamsburg; Cheryl P. Aldridge, Vicars' Deputy for Administration, Old North Church; Ross Urquhart, Print Department, Massachusetts Historical Society; Michael J. Ettema, Curator, Division of Domestic Life, Henry Ford Museum & Greenfield Village; and Anne E. Watkins, Abby Aldrich Rockefeller Folk Center.

I am indebted to Pauline H. Mitchell, Registrar of Shelburne Museum, for all her help. She went out of her way to provide me with many excellent photographs for this book. Ledley Boyce of Paxton Hardware Ltd. is here acknowledged for her patience in developing the bolt-together standard. I also express my gratitude to my photographer, Deborah Porter, for her work in photographing the projects for this book.

Finally, I would like to thank my wife Joyce. She assisted in the preparation of the manuscript and was always supportive.

Wind from the East, bad for man and for beast;
Wind from the South, is too hot for them both;
Wind from the North, is of very little worth;
Wind from the West, is the softest and the best.

The Old Farmer's Almanack, 1851

INTRODUCTION

A weather vane is nothing more than a pointer of some kind, mounted on a spindle, that swings toward the direction from which the wind is blowing. The pointer can be anything from a simple arrow cut out of a piece of pine to an elaborate three-dimensional, copper, gold-leafed, winged eagle.

For a long time I have had a fascination for these simple structures. As a boy in rural New England, I admired the old weather vanes that sat atop most barns across the countryside. Each had a character of its own. Most were larger than those made today. These weather vanes were made by hand, many of them by unskilled local people. The delightful, one-of-a-kind, sometimes crude weather vanes were almost always based on familiar and sentimental themes. No two were alike and some even bordered on the absurd.

In modern New England, however, the countryside is quickly changing, as stately old barns are lost to disrepair, fire, the weight of snow, and of course, to "progress." Weather vanes have almost disappeared from the barns that remain. Just a very few weather vanes still sit atop the buildings on which they were first placed. Among them are the rooster on the First Church in Cambridge, Massachusetts; the banner on the Old North Church in Boston; and the famous copper grasshopper atop Faneuil Hall in Boston. These three were made by hand by Shem Drowne, America's first documented weather vane maker. Some old weather vanes have found sanctuary in museums. Others are now gone from public view: avid collectors use antique weather vanes for wall decorations in the home, as pieces of sculpture, and as garden decorations.

Through the years I have taken or collected photographs, sketches, and drawings of the wonderful old weather vanes throughout the Northeast. Each drawing resembles the original weather vane as closely as possible because I have sought to provide an accurate record of these one-of-a-kind pieces from history. I have included with each weather vane design as much information as I could obtain. In cases where I could not determine the exact size of the original weather vane, as when I was working from an old photograph, I made an educated guess.

Each weather vane pattern is drawn to scale on a square grid so that it can be reproduced in any size. I have provided complete instructions for enlarging or reducing each pattern.

Because many homeowners and apartment dwellers cannot use a weather vane—or can use only one—I have included a few suggestions for other ways to enjoy these wonderful folk-art patterns. They can be made into anything, from simple pull toys for children to bookends. They can even be used for stencil patterns. With a little imagination, you will find dozens of additional uses for these designs.

In writing this book I do not intend to present myself as an expert on weather vanes. For technical or historical information about the subject, readers should refer to a variety of excellent reference books. This book is intended only to record, in scale, some of the original designs and to offer suggestions for their use.

The History of Weather Vanes

Human beings have always wanted to know which way the wind blows. Perhaps early man simply wanted to avoid the smoke from his fires that blew into his face. Knowing wind direction also helped early man to predict the weather, which directly affected most of his daily activities.

The Greeks provided the first record of a weather vane. This weather vane was in the shape of Triton, the half-man, half-fish god of the sea. It stood atop the octagonal Tower of the Winds, which was built in Athens in the first century A.D.

Archaeological evidence demonstrates that early Viking ships also used wind indicators. Weather vanes came to Europe in the Middle Ages. The early European weather vanes reflected the heraldic traditions of medieval castles, often bearing the insignia of the feudal lords.

In colonial America weather vane motifs were limited to a few basic designs: a simple arrow, a rooster or cock, a fish, an Indian, a grasshopper. After the colonies obtained independence from England, designs began to reflect special or local interest. Churches used Christian symbols, such as a cock, a fish, or an angel. Farmers used livestock themes to adorn their houses and barns: horses, cows, sheep, pigs, hens, and roosters. Along the seacoast, fish, whales, ships, and even serpents were popular.

Early originals were made of pine that was carved to the desired form. Later, craftsmen cut thin sheets of iron, zinc, or tin to shape with a hammer and chisel. Even later, weather vanes were made of soft copper or bronze. These usually had hollow bodies. A simple half-mold was carved into a piece of wood and the copper or bronze was beaten into the half-mold. The two halves were then soldered together to create a three-dimensional, hollow body.

Many early hollow-bodied weather vanes contained written messages from their original makers. The name of the maker, the date, the recipient, and other pertinent information about the vane might be included. If the weather vane was repaired, that craftsman might add to the note. Even now, some fortunate owners are finding these messages in their weather vanes.

The local carvers and metalworkers who made these weather vanes were concerned with the functionality of their designs. The pointer's shape had to be broad enough to catch the wind, with more surface area on the side opposite the indicator. A rooster made an excellent pointer: the tail feathers offered a large surface area to the wind, which swung the vane around until the beak pointed into the wind, indicating its direction.

The pointer's shape needed to balance on the pivot point. Hollow-bodied weather vanes were easy to balance. Molten lead could be poured into the hollow body wherever necessary to balance the vane. Flat silhouette designs were slightly harder to balance because of the difficulty in hiding the counterbalance material. Thin strips of lead were attached to the lighter side in such a way as to be nearly invisible from the ground.

An early New England maker of weather vanes was once asked if he could build a weather vane that would indicate the velocity as well as the direction of the wind. The craftsman is reported to have told his customer, "What we use around these parts is a length of chain. When the chain stands out straight, there's a gale a-blowin'." This joke became famous, and in fact, many colonial weather vanes contain a chain somewhere in their structure.

Most early wooden weather vanes were painted white, Indian red, or yellow ocher. The ocher was used to simulate gilt. Some were painted with bold, bright colors. Metal weather vanes were painted or gilded. As for wooden weather vanes, yellow ocher was often used in place of gilt or gold leaf. Some metal vanes were left unpainted, but most had a coat of dark brown or black so that they would create a bold silhouette against the sky. Copper weather vanes were left unpainted and allowed to weather to a beautiful soft gray.

By 1850 or so, most weather vanes were being mass-produced by commercial factories. These early companies issued catalogs illustrating their fine products and designs. With the advent of the industrial age and the development of mechanical machines like the locomotive and steam engine, weather vanes began to use these motifs in their designs. A finely crafted horse weather vane complete with stand and direction letters could be purchased from A. B. and W. T. Westervelt of New York for as little as seventeen dollars—in 1883, of course.

In the 1920s and 1930s, lightning rods became popular in America; they were added to the roof of almost every barn. Round glass balls were attached to each lightning rod spike, probably for ornamentation. It became common practice to slide a weather vane down over the spike, just above the glass ball. The hollow-bodied weather vanes were usually made of zinc and were available in many designs. They were sold to dealers for 54 cents each and usually offered free to the farmer with a contract to add lightning rods to a roof. These 54-cent weather vanes now sell for well over a hundred dollars.

Today, weather vanes are valued antiques. The highest recorded price yet paid for a weather vane is $320,000 for a metal train motif. The price for a very nice weather vane in excellent condition could run from $20,000 to $30,000. Most, however, sell for prices ranging from $1,000 to $7,000. The motifs in greatest demand by collectors are horses, bulls, and cows made between 1840 and 1895.

A page from an 1880 Cushing & White catalog, showing the wide variety of copper weather vanes that were available. The original catalog page can be seen in the Stage Coach Inn at the Shelburne Museum. Courtesy, Shelburne Museum, Shelburne, Vermont.

This weathercock is a full-bodied, three-dimensional weather vane of copper with glass eyes. Thomas Drowne, son of the famous tinsmith Shem, formed the body by carving a reverse model into a piece of wood, then hammering the sheet copper into the mold until it assumed the desired shape. It was completed in 1771 and delivered to the East Church in Salem, Massachusetts. Later it was moved to the Bentley School, built in 1861. In 1953 the weather vane was given to the city of Salem. Courtesy, Essex Institute, Salem, Massachusetts.

This handsome hollow-bodied copper grasshopper is 43 inches long. Notice how the compass points are arranged in two tiers. Old Sturbridge Village photograph.

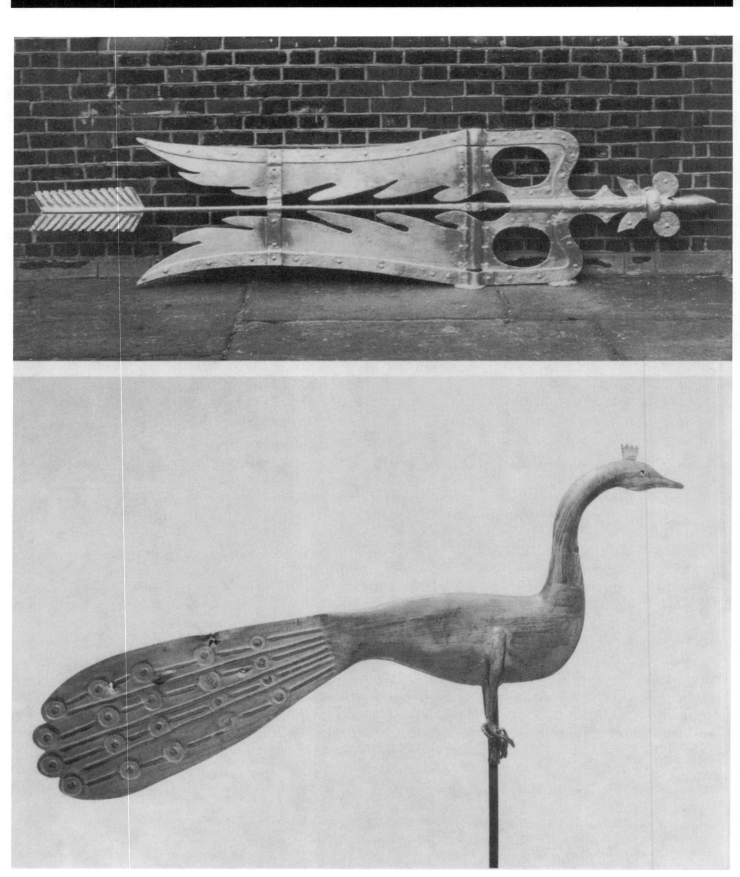

Above: This weather vane, showing Washington on horseback, was made c. 1875. It was cut from ³/₁₆-inch sheet iron and measures only 16½ inches wide and 13½ inches high. Courtesy, Shelburne Museum, Shelburne, Vermont.

Upper left: This beautiful gilt banner usually sits atop Independence Hall in Philadelphia. Made in 1787, it has been repaired twice: once in 1828, and again in 1961, when this photo was taken. Photo courtesy of Independence National Historical Park collection, Philadelphia, Pennsylvania.

Lower left: Made by A.L. Jewell Company c. 1860, this elegant peacock was found in Connecticut. It measures 36½ inches wide and 16 inches high. The lead body is hollow and the intricate tail is made from copper. (The A.L. Jewell Company was later acquired by Cushing & White.) Courtesy, Shelburne Museum, Shelburne, Vermont.

This rooster weather vane from Pennsylvania measures 32 inches high and 30 inches wide. It is composed of several sections of pine that are glued together and secured by iron strips. It is painted on both sides: its body is black, the eyes are yellow, and its comb, crest, and mouth are red. Courtesy, Shelburne Museum, Shelburne, Vermont.

The naturalistic butterfly, discovered in Connecticut, was fashioned out of sheet copper. The copper was hammered and pierced to suggest color patterns. It measures 27½ inches wide and 19 inches high. Courtesy, Shelburne Museum, Shelburne, Vermont.

This 32-inch banner from the Friedberg Church dates back to c. 1825. Courtesy, Old Salem Restoration, Winston-Salem, North Carolina.

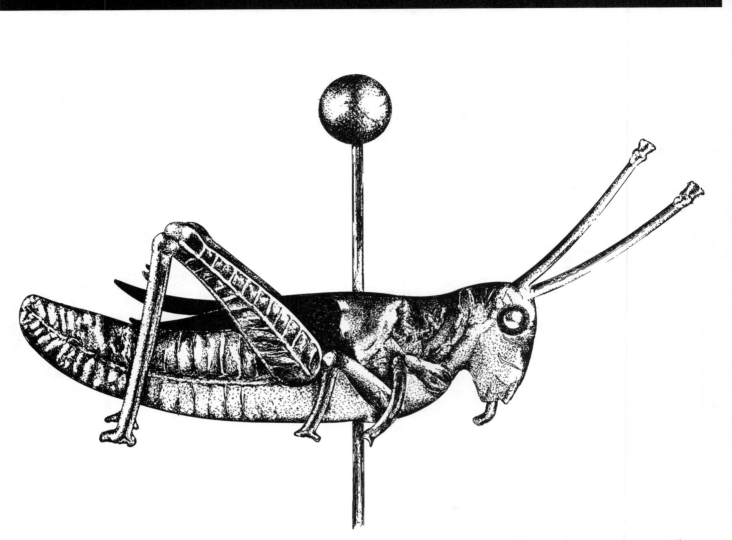

One of Boston's most famous landmarks, this huge golden grasshopper twirls majestically atop historic Faneuil Hall. As the oldest weather vane in continuous use in the United States, it has brought acclaim to its maker, master tinsmith Deacon Shem Drowne. Drowne fashioned the grasshopper out of sheet copper in 1742, using green glass for the eyes.

Faneuil Hall has always been a farmer's market. So why would farmers choose to honor the grasshopper, a scourge to the farming community since biblical times? No one knows for certain, but one theory has considerable popularity.

It is said that in the year 1519 a group of children chasing grasshoppers in a field outside of London found an abandoned baby in the grass. They took the infant to a nearby church, where he was sheltered. He grew up to become Sir Thomas Gresham, financial adviser to Queen Elizabeth and founder of the Royal Exchange. As a token of his gratitude, Sir Thomas had a grasshopper placed on the Exchange building.

A few centuries later, Peter Faneuil became a member of this same exchange. He was fascinated by both the shape of the building's weather vane and the story of its origin. Years later, Faneuil came to America. He settled in Boston, and as his business began to thrive he built Faneuil Hall, which he gave to the city for use as a general market. It is certainly possible that he arranged for a grasshopper weather vane to be placed on the building, but this theory lacks documentation and may be nothing more than romantic speculation.

Another tale involving this famous weather vane concerns a U.S. consul from Boston who was stationed in Glasgow in 1780. He was approached by three sailors without identification papers. The trio said they were U.S. citizens from Boston, stranded and in need of fare to get home. The diplomat reportedly pulled each man aside and asked him to describe the weather vane of Faneuil Hall. Two of them were unable to do so. "Anyone who claims to be a Bostonian and who does not know the shape of the hall's weather vane must be an imposter," said the consul. "You can walk home." The third sailor answered correctly and received his fare.

This weather vane was made of two pieces of sheet metal pressed together and then painted gold. The motif measures 39 inches wide and 27 inches high. It portrays a Native American legend about a tribe that kept a mountain lion as a pet. The lion attacked the horse of the chieftain and so the chieftain slew the lion. The members of the tribe were so angry they expelled the chieftain from their tribe forever. Courtesy, Shelburne Museum, Shelburne, Vermont.

This banner weather vane (**left** and **right**) was made by Jacob Eckfelt in 1824 for Congress Hall, which was completed in 1791. **Right:** The banner has been regilded and is about to be mounted. Photos courtesy of Independence National Historical Park collection, Philadelphia, Pennsylvania.

The rooster was a favorite motif for old-time makers of weather vanes. This example has been dated to c. 1845. In a very primitive style, it was cut from a single piece of 1¹/₈-inch pine, with the addition of another piece for the tail feathers. Dimensions are 31 inches long by 17 inches high. Courtesy, Shelburne Museum, Shelburne, Vermont.

23

Very little is known of the history of this sheet-metal cow. Courtesy, Shelburne Museum, Shelburne, Vermont.

Upper left: Amazing craftsmanship accounts for the fine detail in this copper weather vane. Believed to have been copied directly from a full-size fire engine, it was used on the local firehouse in Manchester, New Hampshire. Courtesy, Shelburne Museum, Shelburne, Vermont.

Lower left: This handsome carved weather vane is attributed to James Lombard, who was born in Baldwin, Maine, in 1865. He made his living as a farmer and carved weather vanes for pleasure. Courtesy, Shelburne Museum, Shelburne, Vermont.

This eagle silhouette, found in Connecticut, measures 24½ inches wide and 17 inches high. It was cut from a single sheet of iron. Courtesy, Shelburne Museum, Shelburne, Vermont.

This weather vane measures 36 inches wide and 16½ inches high. It was cut from sheet iron and then painted. The rider is said to be Paul Revere. Courtesy, Shelburne Museum, Shelburne, Vermont.

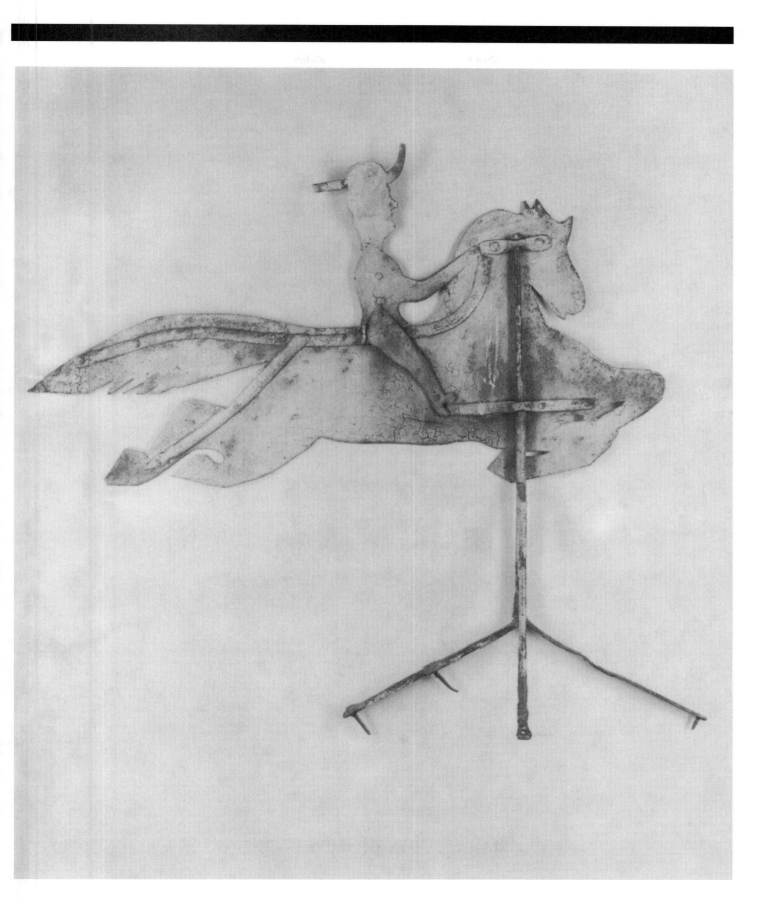

This beautiful banner comes from the Moravian Church in Winston-Salem, North Carolina. It was made in 1788 by Matthaeus Oesterlein (1752–1798), a local blacksmith and the church organist. The banner measures 60 inches long and 13 inches high, and the ball is 2½ feet in diameter. Courtesy, Old Salem Restoration, Winston-Salem, North Carolina.

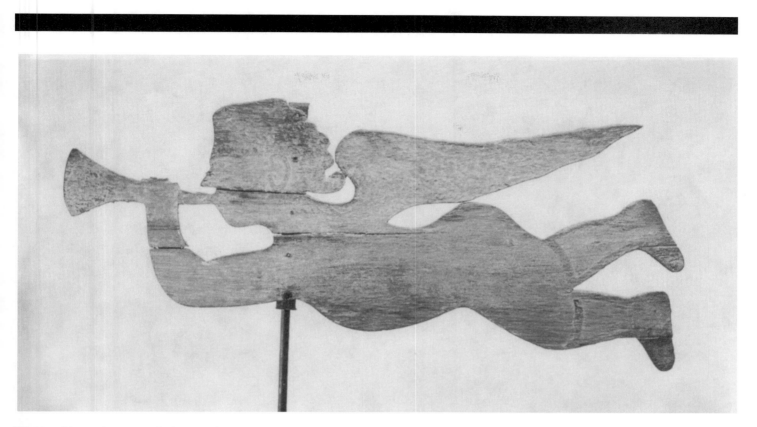

This cherubic angel was carved of pine and painted white c. 1800. It measures 33 1/2 inches long and 13 inches high. It was found in Ridgefield, Connecticut, and is thought to be the work of an amateur. Courtesy, Shelburne Museum, Shelburne, Vermont.

This trotting-horse weather vane (c. 1880) measures 24 inches high and 51 1/2 inches wide. Made of copper, it is gilded and has a beautiful blue-green patina. From the collections of Henry Ford Museum & Greenfield Village.

Fashioned of pine with iron reinforcements, this attractive weather vane measures 46 inches high and 39 inches wide. It was found in Westfield, New York. Notice the detail in the Indian's feather headdress and the foliage beneath him. Courtesy, The Henry Francis du Pont Winterthur Museum.

This silhouette of a deer is made of iron and measures 22 inches high. The vertical and horizontal straps make the weather vane more rigid and provide support to the slender legs. The crudely shaped tail and antlers indicate primitive work. Courtesy, Shelburne Museum, Shelburne, Vermont.

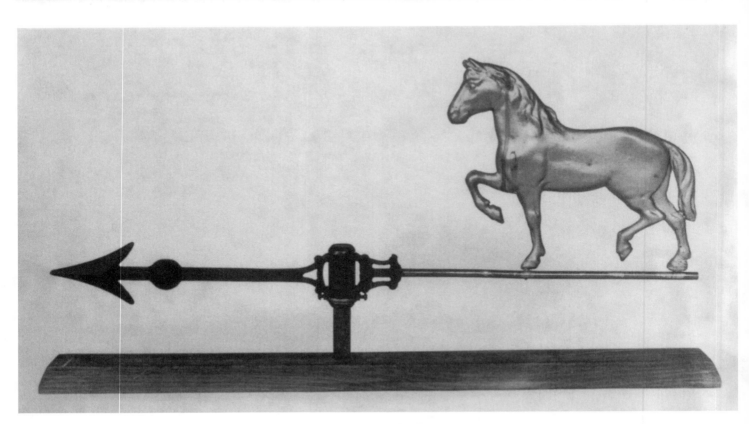

Top: The arrow of this lightning rod weather vane (c. 1936) measures 24 inches long. The small horse is 9 inches wide and 7½ inches high and is painted a glossy gold. It survives by happy accident, having been removed from a barn in St. Johnsbury Center, Vermont, a month before the barn was completely destroyed by fire.

Right: This rooster is an excellent example of an early carved weather vane. It is 41 inches long and 33 inches high and dates to c. 1790. Courtesy, Shelburne Museum, Shelburne, Vermont.

Far right: This very early (c. 1670) weathercock is from Europe, probably southern Germany. The entire structure is made of iron and measures 82½ inches high and 36 inches wide. Only the figure at the top revolves. Notice the engraving on the horizontal piece. Courtesy, The Henry Francis du Pont Winterthur Museum.

This crowing cock is a fine example of a weather vane cut to shape from sheet iron. It has been painted to give the effect of three dimensions. It measures 20½ inches wide and 19 inches high. Although it was found in Mechanicsville, New York, it is said to be from Massachusetts. Courtesy, Shelburne Museum, Shelburne, Vermont.

This weather vane, found in Pennsylvania, was cut c. 1810 from sheet iron ¹/₁₆-inch thick. It is 51 inches high and 31 inches wide. The meaning of the mysterious *TO,TE* inscription is yet undiscovered. Courtesy, Shelburne Museum, Shelburne, Vermont.

This finely detailed, three-dimensional weather
vane was made of copper and brass by Cushing &
White of Waltham, Massachusetts c. 1880.
From the collections of Henry Ford Museum &
Greenfield Village.

Enlarging or Reducing a Pattern

It is important that your weather vane be an appropriate size for the building on which it will sit. So many inexpensive commercially made weather vanes mounted today are much too small—not even large enough to adorn a doghouse. Top-quality commercially made weather vanes priced from $500 to $1,000 or more are usually the correct size for most modern homes. Making your own weather vane, however, permits you to have the appropriate size and avoid paying a high price.

A general rule for the size of a weather vane is that it should be one inch in width or height (whichever is larger) for every one foot in distance from the ground to the place it will be mounted. In figure 1, for example, the roof peak is twenty-two feet above ground; therefore the weather vane should be a minimum of twenty-two inches wide or twenty-two inches high. A smaller vane would look out of place; a slightly larger one would probably be acceptable. For a one-story home, a weather vane of eighteen inches is about right; for a two-story house, figure on thirty-two inches.

Once you have selected a design and figured out the appropriate size, you will need to enlarge or reduce the pattern to that size. The patterns in this book are based as closely as possible on the silhouettes of the original weather vanes, so you will want to be careful not to distort the shape as you enlarge or reduce.

One of the simplest and most inexpensive ways to alter the size of a pattern is to use a photocopier. Newer machines include a feature that enlarges or reduces. Simply choose the enlargement or reduction mode and make a copy. For extreme reductions or enlargements, the process might take two or more steps; reduce the reduction (or enlarge the enlargement) until you get the size you want.

Another quick method, one that is extremely accurate, is to get a PMT, or photomechanical transfer, made at a local printing shop. This photographic method can provide exact enlargements or reductions of the design without any effort on your part. Prices will range from $5 to $15, depending on the size of the final PMT. If your time is valuable, this method might be worth the cost.

Another simple, quick method is to use a drawing tool called a pantograph. The pantograph's adjustable arms can enlarge or reduce to most any size. If you do a lot of enlarging or reducing, this tool may be well worth its modest price ($5 to $15).

The method most often used by woodworkers is the grid and dot-to-dot. It is very simple, doesn't require the skills of an artist, and can be used to enlarge or reduce to any size or scale. A few basic drafting tools, including a drafting board, a scale (a simple ruler will do), a T-square, a 45-degree triangle, and masking tape would be helpful, but you can im-

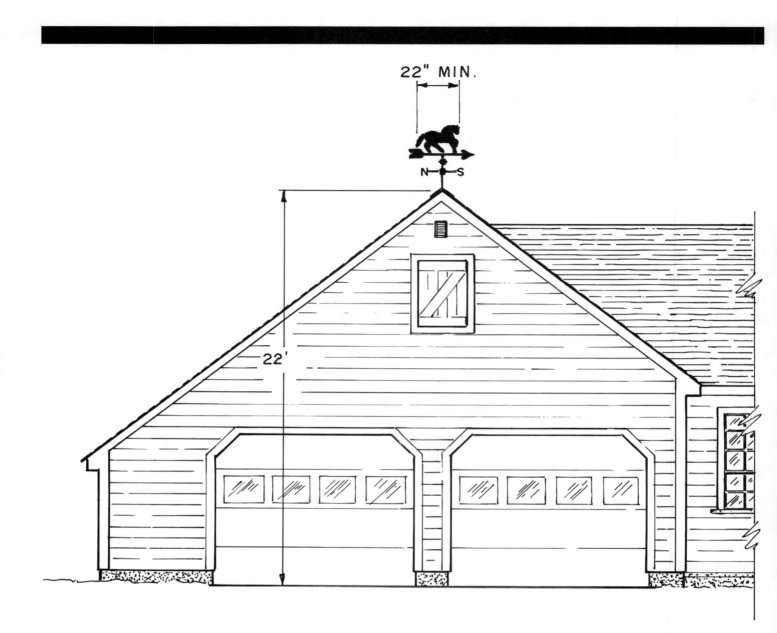

FIGURE I. Make sure that the size of your motif is appropriate for the size of the structure on which it will be mounted.

provise with what you have at home. Follow these seven steps to adapt any pattern to the size you want.

Step 1. Decide on either the width or the height, in inches, you want for the finished project. Divide that number by the number of grid lines for that dimension in the pattern. This number will be the size of the grid for your project. In this example (see figure 2) the width of this portion of the finished project will be 7½ inches. There are 10 vertical lines in the original. So 7.5 divided by 10 gives you .75. Therefore, you will need a grid of 10 lines, ¾ inch apart. Notice that all you have to do is figure one dimension. Since the grid is square, the horizontal lines must be the same distance apart as the vertical lines.

Step 2. Tape your paper to the drafting board and carefully draw the required grid.

Step 3. On the original pattern, start from the upper left corner and number the squares from left to right. From the same starting point, use letters on the vertical axis. In this example, the numbers run horizontally

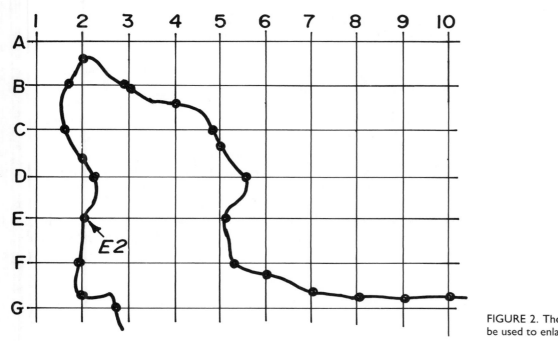

FIGURE 2. The grid and dot-to-dot method can be used to enlarge or reduce a pattern.

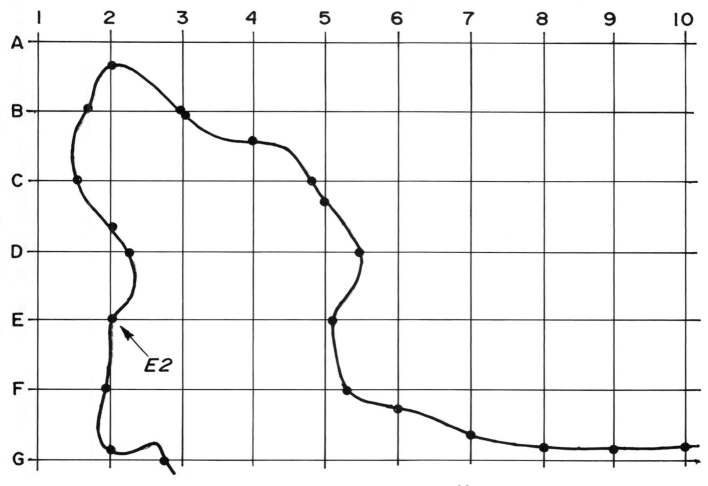

along the top from 1 through 10 and the letters go from A through G.

    Step 4. On your full-size grid, mark letters and numbers the same way.

    Step 5. On the original drawing, mark dots along the pattern outline wherever it crosses a line.

    Step 6. On your full-size grid, carefully locate and draw dots corresponding to the ones you marked on the original. Be sure to use the numbers and letters to guide you.

    Step 7. Connect the dots. You do not have to be exact. Simply sketch lines between the dots. Do not forget to draw the location of the mounting hole in the pattern.

    If you intend to make several pieces from the same pattern, transfer the pattern to a sheet of heavy cardboard or 1/8-inch hardboard or plywood and cut it out. You can simply retrace around this template to make copies.

Making a Weather Vane

After you have a full-size pattern, you will need to decide what material you want to use for your weather vane. Weather vanes crafted from patterns in this book can be made of wood, sheet metal, aluminum, plastic, or whatever else you have available. Your selection may be limited by what tools you have to work with.

WOOD

Two general kinds of wood are available: softwoods, such as pine, spruce, and cedar; and hardwoods, such as maple, oak, ash, basswood, and walnut. Softwoods weigh less than hardwoods and are easier to work with, and since the standard assembly—the support on which a vane is mounted—is rather light, pine would be a good choice. If you are concerned with authenticity, choose pine, the wood most often used by early craftsmen. If you prefer a hardwood, I suggest basswood, which like pine is easy to work with. Exterior-grade plywood is also an excellent choice, but of course, it lacks authenticity.

Whichever variety you choose, be sure to get well-seasoned, knot-free wood with a straight grain. The thickness of the wood you select will depend on what kind of weather vane you want. Use ½-inch wood for a thin silhouette weather vane, and 1½-inch for a carved pattern. If the pattern is so large that you must glue pieces of wood together, be sure to use a high-quality, weatherproof glue; your weather vane will be out in the elements for many years.

To transfer the pattern from paper to wood, place a sheet of carbon paper between the pattern and the wood. Pay close attention to the direction of the grain; so that the wood won't crack and break, position the thin areas of the pattern, such as an animal's legs, parallel to the grain. Then tape the pattern in place and trace it. Again, remember to locate and draw the location and direction of the mounting hole.

If the pattern is symmetrical—the exact same size and shape on both sides of a line that bisects the pattern—make only half a pattern and trace it twice, once on each side of a line you draw on the wood. This will ensure perfect symmetry of the finished project.

Should it be necessary, larger sizes of carbon paper just for woodworkers (seventeen by twenty-two inches) can be purchased from Meisel Hardware Specialties (refer to No. 7347 when ordering).

Another transfer method is to make a photocopy of the pattern. Then tape the copy, printed side down, to the wood. Using a hot flatiron or wood-burning set, heat the back side of the copy; the pattern will be

Carved motifs have a special charm. To keep your weather vane balanced, make symmetrical reductions on the front and back.

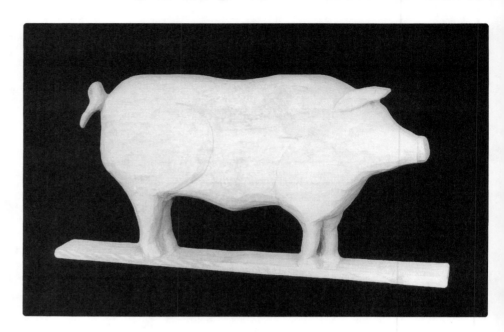

transferred from the paper directly to the wood. This works well for very small, complicated patterns.

Carefully cut out the weather vane, keeping all cuts at 90 degrees to the surface. If your weather vane is a silhouette, sand all edges, keeping a 90-degree angle.

Locate and drill the mounting hole for the shaft. Be sure to drill in the exact center of the board and at the exact same angle as on the pattern. Use a doweling jig if you have one; it will help position the hole in the exact center of the board. Take care to drill this hole precisely as shown. If it is not located in just the right spot, the weather vane will not rotate correctly.

If you plan to carve your weather vane, it is a good idea to draw a line in pencil an inch or so inside all edges. This will provide a reference point for making symmetrical reductions at all borders. You need only two carving tools: a No. 5 gouge (12 mm) and a No. 12 V-groove (8 mm). To get the best results, use high-quality carving tools and keep them very sharp at all times. Then, think of yourself as a crafter from two hundred years ago and let your imagination take over.

METAL AND OTHER MATERIALS

Many early weather vanes were made from thin iron, which may be difficult to get today. Aluminum and copper are readily available and are also relatively lightweight. Your weather vane can be made of almost anything, but remember that the heavier your weather vane is, the more difficult it will be to mount.

Steel sheet metal (16 or 18 gauge) will work, but you must have a band or scroll saw outfitted with a metal-cutting blade. Sheet metal is much more difficult to cut than wood and demands much more care when you're making motifs and letters. I made a steel weather vane using my scroll saw set at a very slow speed. The project used a lot of blades and was very time consuming. Early craftsmen are said to have chiseled their patterns out of raw iron sheets; that must have been quite a chore.

To transfer the patterns to metal, simply place a sheet of carbon paper between the pattern and the metal and trace over it. You can also make a template of cardboard and trace around it. Don't try the ironing method on metal.

The availability of metals with low melting temperatures might lead you to try casting a weather vane. Read up on simple casting methods before you attempt it.

FINISHING

Wood

You can make a new wooden weather vane look old by leaving it—unpainted—out in the elements for a few months. Before long it ages to a pleasing soft gray. To stop the weathering process, apply two coats of satin-finish exterior varnish.

An antique effect can be achieved by lightly scorching all surfaces with a propane torch. (Do this outdoors with a bucket of water handy in case of fire.) This technique will give your weather vane that hundred-year-old look and will actually help preserve the wood. Scour the wood all over, with the grain, using a steel-wire brush. Then mount it unfinished, or apply a coat of paint or transparent preservative to the brushed wood. Either way your weather vane will look mellowed and antique.

Don't forget that some early weather vanes were painted in bright colors. Use your imagination—you can always repaint if you don't like what you end up with. Oil-based primer and paint will do the best job of preserving your handiwork.

Metal

Primer and two or three coats of oil-based paint (brown and black are most authentic) should be applied to weather vanes made of steel or aluminum. Before applying the finish, sand the metal parts to rough up the surface so that the primer and paint will adhere correctly. A copper weather vane will age with exposure to the elements, but you can make it look older immediately by coating it with copper sulfate and acetic acid.

Making the Standard

The weather vane motif or design is mounted on an assembly called a standard. The standard is made up of the roof stand or base, a main shaft, a support for the compass points, a stamped ball, a pointer, and a support shaft for the motif. Figure 3 gives the sizes for various parts of the standard.

Not all weather vane assemblies contain all these components. Before building your weather vane, you must decide which to include in your project. Figures 4–7 illustrate some of the various combinations you can use. Be sure you know where true north is located before you decide to leave off the compass points. Homeowners may have found it easier to pinpoint compass directions in years past, when it was customary to build a house or barn in direct relationship to the points of the compass.

A standard can be made in several ways, using many different materials. If you have access to a welder, you may want to weld your standard together. The suggested standard is designed to be made with very few tools. It requires only a tape measure, a hacksaw, an adjustable wrench, and a small pipe cutter. If you don't have a pipe cutter, you can use the hacksaw. The whole assembly is simply cut to size and bolted together. The plans in figure 8 call for rivets, but No. 4 brass machine screws and nuts can be substituted.

Parts for the standard can be purchased separately from local hardware or lamp stores, but I suggest that you order all parts from one source. Paxton Hardware Ltd., 7818 Bradshaw Road, Upper Falls, Maryland

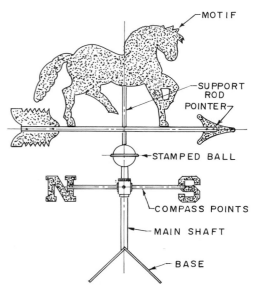

The base, the main shaft, and the support rod are the backbone of the weather vane. The compass points and the pointer make it functional, and the motif and stamped ball add charm.

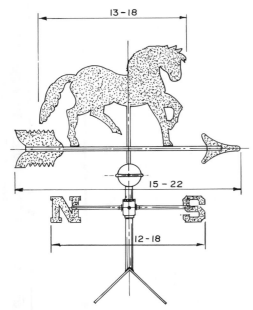

FIGURE 3. This is a complete weather vane with all standard components. Notice that the pointer span is longer than the span of the compass points.

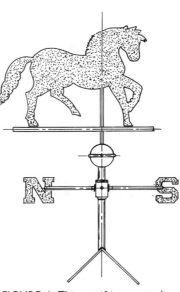

FIGURE 4. This motif is mounted on a shaft without the arrowhead and feathers. To maintain balance, the support rod must be attached farther forward.

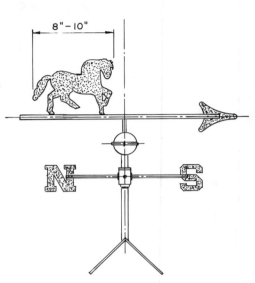

FIGURE 5. This weather vane includes the pointer but lacks the compass points designating north, south, east, and west.

FIGURE 6. Here the motif is reduced and placed at the end of the arrow, where it functions as the tail. This design was used in inexpensive lightning rod weather vanes popular during the 1920s and 1930s.

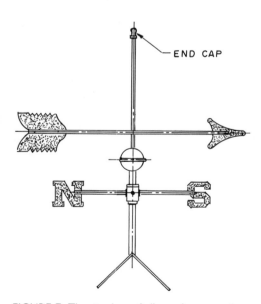

FIGURE 7. The simplest of all weather vanes is the arrow with tail feathers.

21156, can send the required parts as a kit (No. 8730). Call them at (301) 592-8505 for prices.

Study the standard plan and read all the instructions. Be sure you understand how the standard is assembled before you begin. You can change the standard slightly to fit your individual design.

Note that the motif, arrowhead and tails, and direction letters should already be made. If you do not wish to make them out of metal, they can be made of plywood or wood—use whatever materials you are comfortable with. Figure 9 shows some patterns for the arrow and the compass points. Some of these designs require modification to the standard plans. Experiment and see what works.

Remember that this standard is rather lightweight and cannot be used for a thick, heavy motif. A stronger standard must be designed for a heavy weather vane.

Cut all parts to size according to the plans and check that the nuts will thread over the new cuts. File the cut ends lightly, if necessary, so that the standard will fit together easily at assembly time.

Cut a roof support (part No. 1) from 16-gauge metal and bend it to match the roof pitch where the weather vane will be mounted. Drill a ½-inch hole in the center to accept part No. 2.

Assemble the roof support as shown in figure 8. Attach part No. 1 to parts No. 2 and No. 3 using two knurled locknuts (part No. 4), two lockwashers (part No. 5), and two hex nuts (part No. 6). Assemble the parts so that the top of part No. 2 is in the center of the four holes in the four-sided cluster (part No. 7). Tighten all nuts, starting with the top

	PART	SIZE	NEEDED
1	roof support, 16-gauge metal	4 in. × 6 in.	1
2	¼ IP all-thread pipe	12 in.	1
3	¾ OD solid brass tubing	9 in.	1
4	¼ IPF knurled locknut		2
5	¼ IP slip lockwasher		2
6	¼ IPF hex locknut		2
7	brass four-sided cluster		1
8	solid brass ball, ½-in. diam.		1
9	⅛ IP all-thread pipe	7¾ in.	1
10	½ OD solid brass tubing	2¾ in.	1
11	two-piece brass ball, 2-in. diam.		1
12	½ OD solid brass tubing	2¼ in.	1
13	⅛ IP lockwasher		6
14	⅛ IPF hex locknut		6
15	⅛ IP all-thread pipe	9 in.	1
16	¼ OD brass half-hard rod	14 in.	1

Parts 2–16 can be purchased as kit 8730 from Paxton Hardware Ltd.

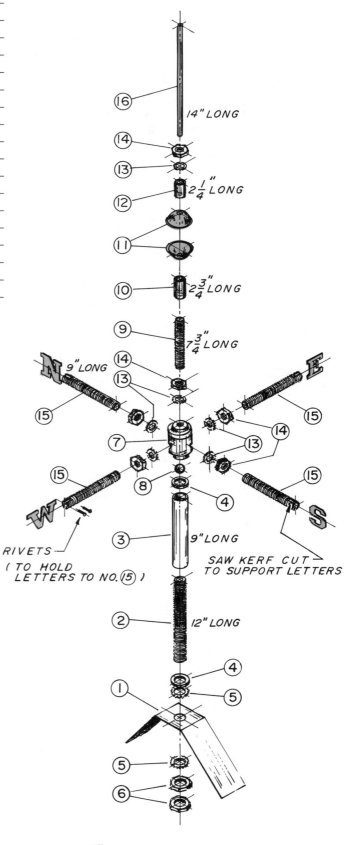

FIGURE 8. This blow-up of the standard assembly (Paxton Hardware kit no. 8730) shows how all the pieces fit together. You may need to modify the plan to accommodate your design changes.

47

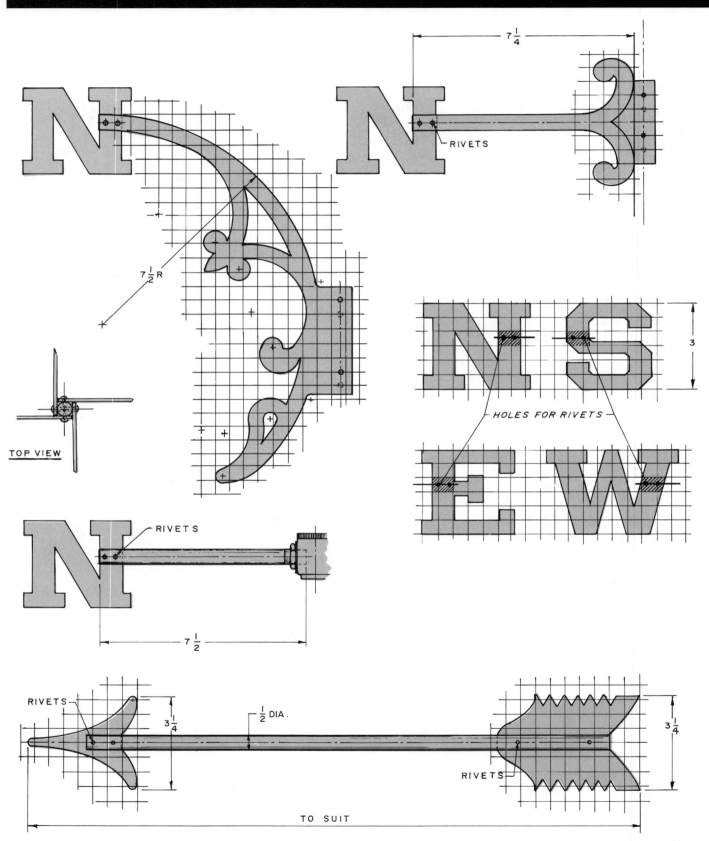

FIGURE 9. These are just a few alternatives for the pointer and the compass points. You may want to design your own.

knurled nut (part No. 4) and moving down to the two bottom hex nuts. The main shaft (part No. 2) will extend 2 or 3 inches below the roof support. This can be trimmed off later if necessary.

Add the ½-inch diameter ball (part No. 8), so that it sits on top of part No. 2. Screw the top pipe (part No. 9) into the cap of the four-sided cluster (part No. 7) and down tightly against the ball. Add a lockwasher (part No. 13) and a hex nut (part No. 14) to lock the top pipe in place. Slip the bottom spacer (part No. 10), the 2-inch diameter brass ball (part No. 11), and the top spacer (part No. 12) over the top pipe, as shown. Lock them all in place with a lockwasher and a hex nut. Trim off the top of the top pipe if it sticks out more than ¼ inch.

Attach the letters N, S, E, and W to the compass supports by making saw cuts about ½ inch in from one end and riveting or screwing the letters to the brass supports (part No. 15) as shown in figures 8 and 9.

Add the compass supports (part No. 15) to the four-sided cluster (part No. 7) using lockwashers (part No. 13) and hex nuts (part No. 14). Be sure to lock them in place in the correct order and position. If possible, try to find solid brass tubing that is threaded ¾ inch in from one end in place of the threaded rod as shown.

Your motif is attached to the ¼-inch-diameter top rod (part No. 16) in one of three ways. If your motif is made of thin metal, attach it to the top rod as shown in figure 10, using either rivets or No. 4 screws and nuts. Secure a motif that is almost as thick as the top rod by constructing simple clips and riveting or screwing them as shown in figure 11. To attach a thick weather vane motif, simply drill a ¼-inch-diameter hole up from

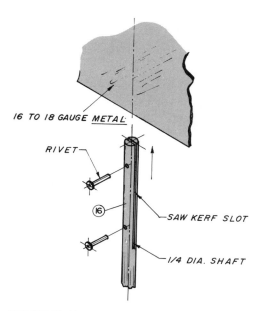

FIGURE 10. To attach a metal motif, make a slot in the top rod and fit the motif in the slot.

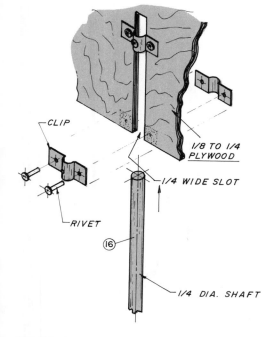

FIGURE 11. Use clips to attach a plywood motif to the top rod.

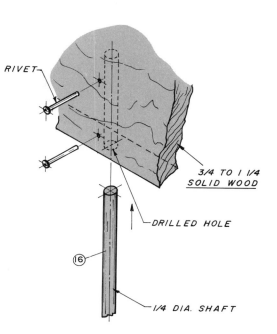

FIGURE 12. For thicker wood motifs, you can simply drill a hole to accept the top rod.

49

Your completed weather vane is attractive and functional and will provide you with years of enjoyment.

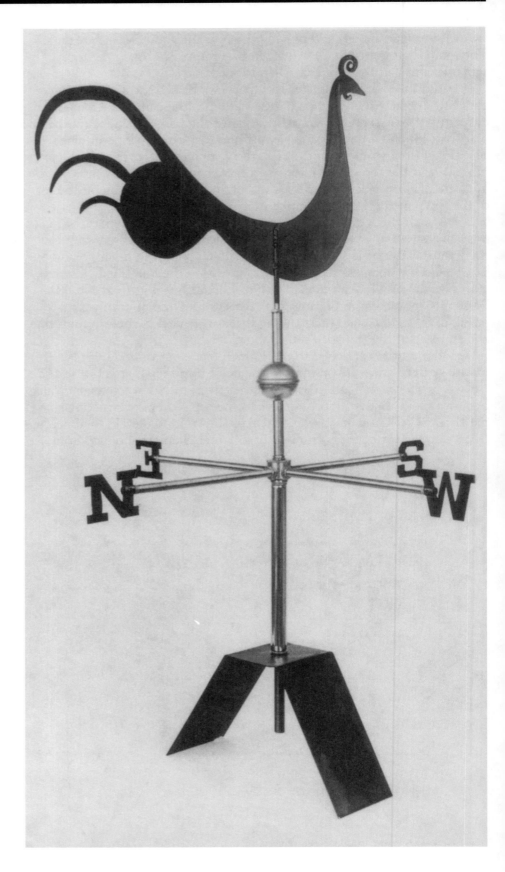

the bottom of the motif, as shown in figure 12, and rivet or screw it to the top rod.

It is very important that you attach the motif to the shaft exactly where indicated on the pattern. There should be a little more area behind the motif than in front of it. If your motif is very heavy on one side of the top rod, add lead weights to the other side for balance.

Note that the completed motif should not extend above the top of the top pipe (part No. 9) more than one inch or so. If necessary, cut the top rod (part No. 16) accordingly. The bottom of the top rod should come in point-contact with the ½-inch-diameter ball (part No. 8), but there should not be much friction. The rod should turn very easily with no drag whatsoever. If there is any friction, find the source of the problem and adjust accordingly. Do not grease or oil the top rod. Grease will cause it to freeze and lock in place in cold weather. Finally, prime and paint the hardware so that it complements your motif.

Now you must attach your weather vane to your roof. It has to be very secure so that it will not blow off the roof in a strong wind. Use heavy-duty bolts and fasten the roof support to the roof in at least two places. Once you are convinced that it is fixed in place, climb down and admire your handiwork.

Other Uses for Weather Vane Patterns

Not everyone needs a weather vane, and very few people need more than one. But weather vane patterns can be used in many other ways. Try some of the projects below or use your imagination to develop a few of your own. Use these wonderful old patterns whenever you need an authentic primitive design. They can even be used for projects such as stencils and quilt appliqués.

The twelve simple projects that follow are all made from the patterns in this book.

Cutting board: weather vane No. 48 enlarged to 11 by 17 inches (a 1-inch grid was used). Use ½-inch to ¾-inch hardwood. Do not apply shellac or varnish to finish it; use a nontoxic oil finish instead. In this example, the edges were painted to highlight the design.

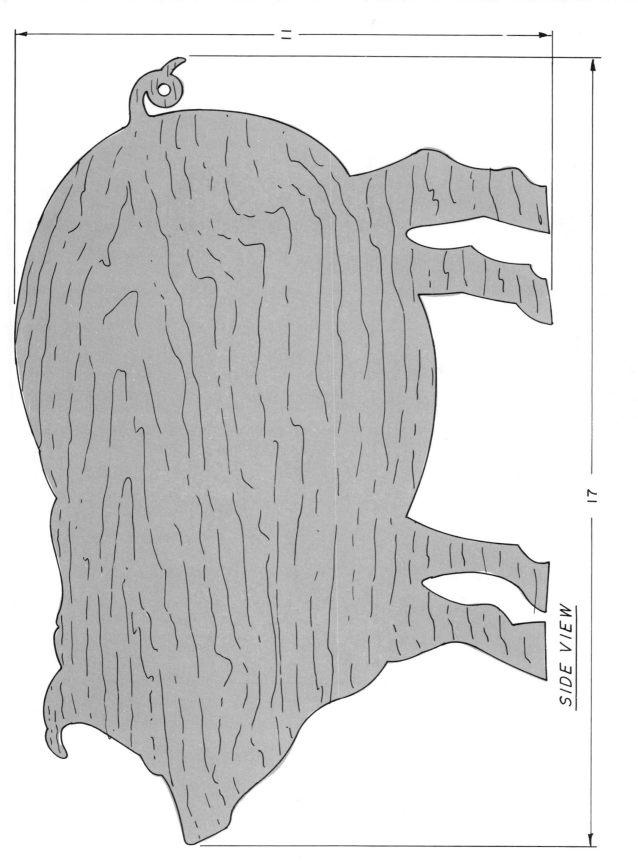

SIDE VIEW

Decorative folk art project: weather vane No. 34, 4¾ by 10 inches (a ¼-inch grid was used). Cut the pattern from ⅜-inch softwood and then stain or paint it. A 2¼-inch-square hardwood block provided the stand, and a welding rod, cut to size, was used as the post.

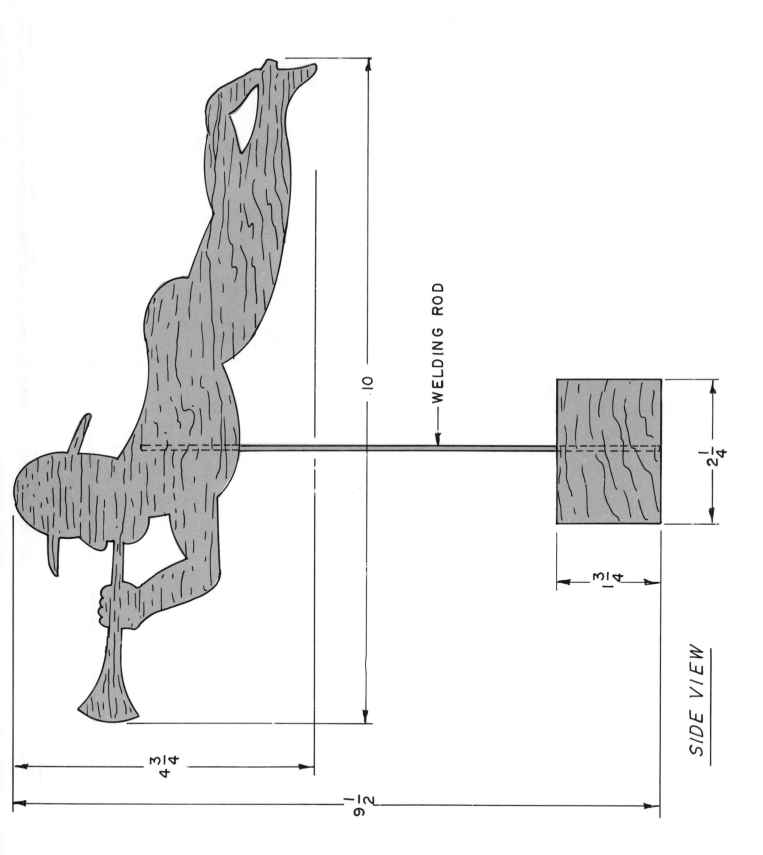

WELDING ROD

10

$2\frac{1}{4}$

$1\frac{3}{4}$

$4\frac{3}{4}$

$9\frac{1}{2}$

SIDE VIEW

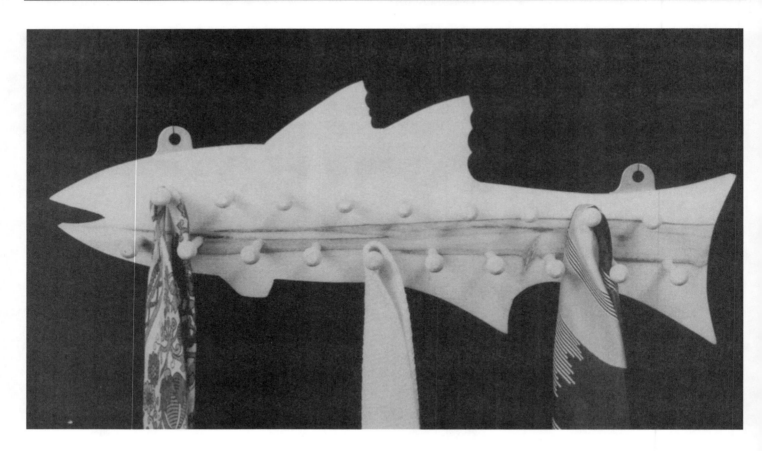

Tie rack: weather vane No. 21 enlarged to 5¼ by 14 inches (a ½-inch grid was used). I built the rack with ½-inch hardwood, although a softwood could be used. The tie rack pegs can be purchased from most woodworking supply houses. Use a light stain, followed by a coat or two of shellac.

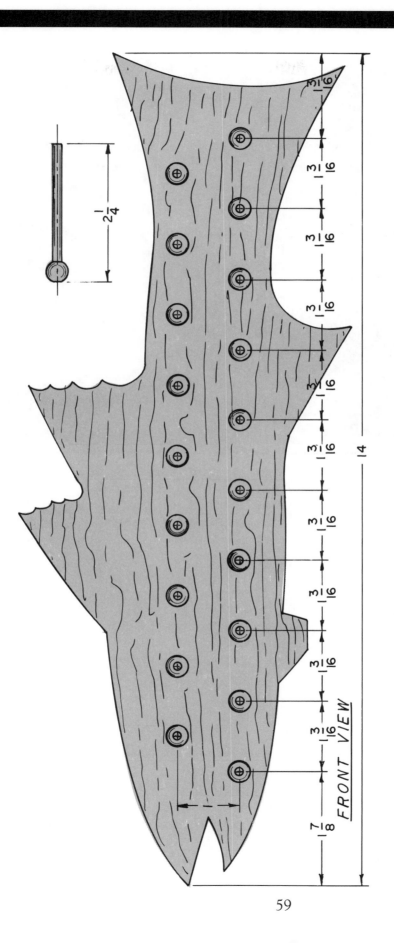

FRONT VIEW

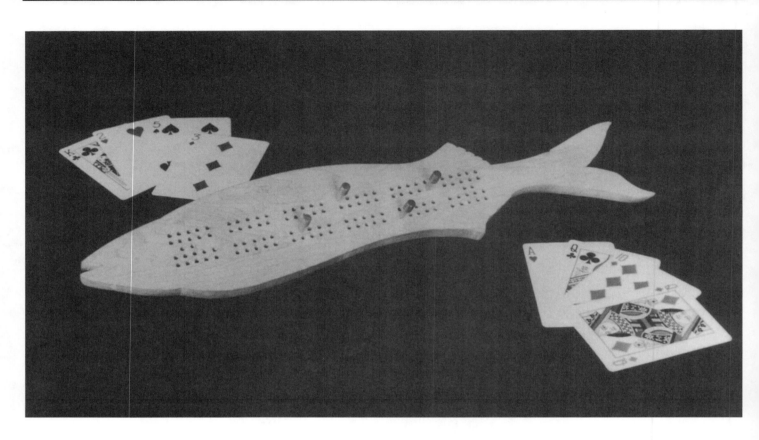

Cribbage board: weather vane pattern No. 17 enlarged to 3 by 15 inches (a ½-inch grid was used). The board can be constructed of ½-inch to ¾-inch hardwood. Carefully lay out and drill the 124 holes, each ⅛ inch in diameter, as shown. Use a light stain, followed by a coat of shellac.

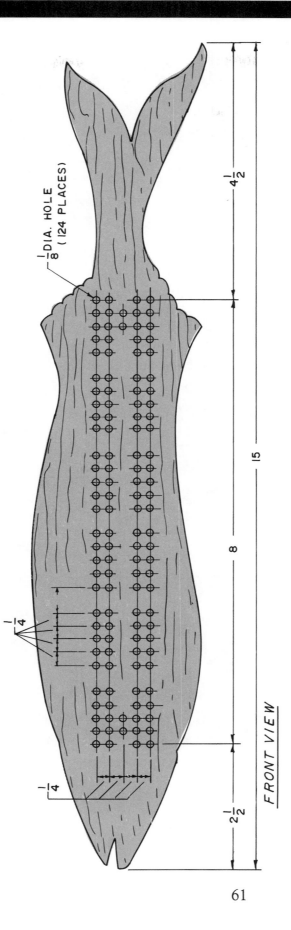

FRONT VIEW

$\frac{1}{8}$ DIA. HOLE
(124 PLACES)

$\frac{1}{4}$

$\frac{1}{4}$

$4\frac{1}{2}$

15

8

$2\frac{1}{2}$

Pull toy: weather vane No. 37, 6½ by 9 inches (a ¼-inch grid was used). This toy is made of ¾-inch hardwood. The wheels are 2 inches in diameter. If the toy will be used by children, be sure to use nontoxic paint and to assemble the toy so that it cannot come apart.

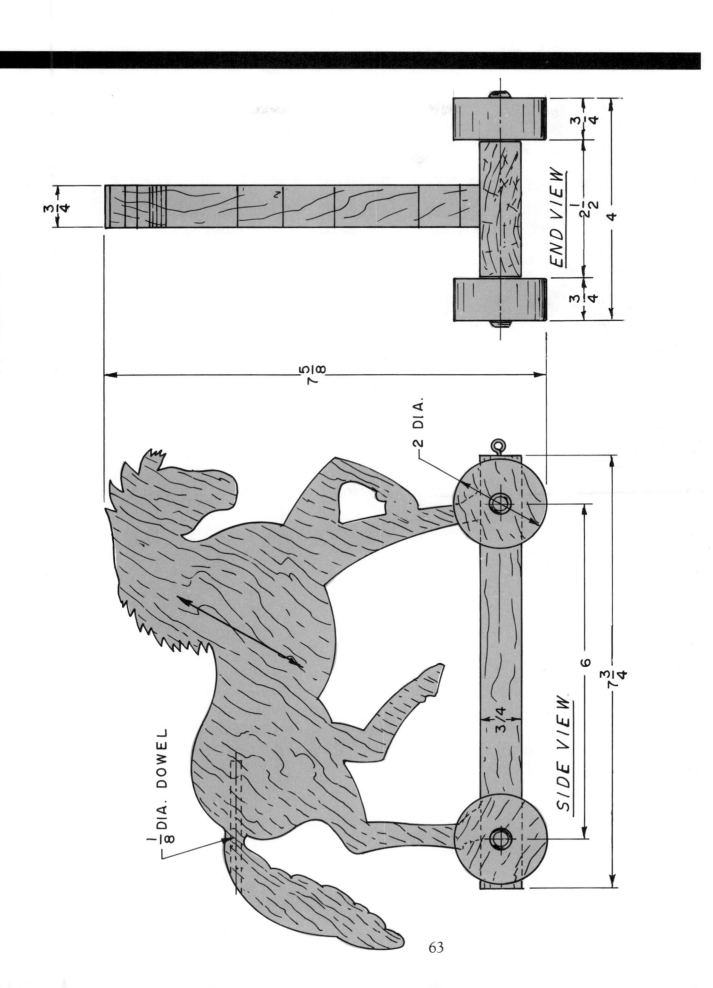

$\frac{3}{4}$

$\frac{3}{4}$

$2\frac{1}{2}$

4

$\frac{3}{4}$

END VIEW

$7\frac{5}{8}$

2 DIA.

6

$7\frac{3}{4}$

3/4

SIDE VIEW

$\frac{1}{8}$ DIA. DOWEL

Christmas tree ornaments: weather vane patterns Nos. 8, 29, 62, 37, 61, and 50, reduced to about 3 inches in diameter. These are cut with a jig-saw from 1/8-inch hardwood with a straight grain. Use a clear finish or paint them with bright colors. They can be hung on the tree with string loops.

Clock: weather vane shown on page 18 enlarged to 14 by 14½ inches (a ½-inch grid was used). Cut the pattern from ¾-inch hardwood and hollow out a place for the clock. The quartz-movement clock shown is 2¾ inches in diameter.

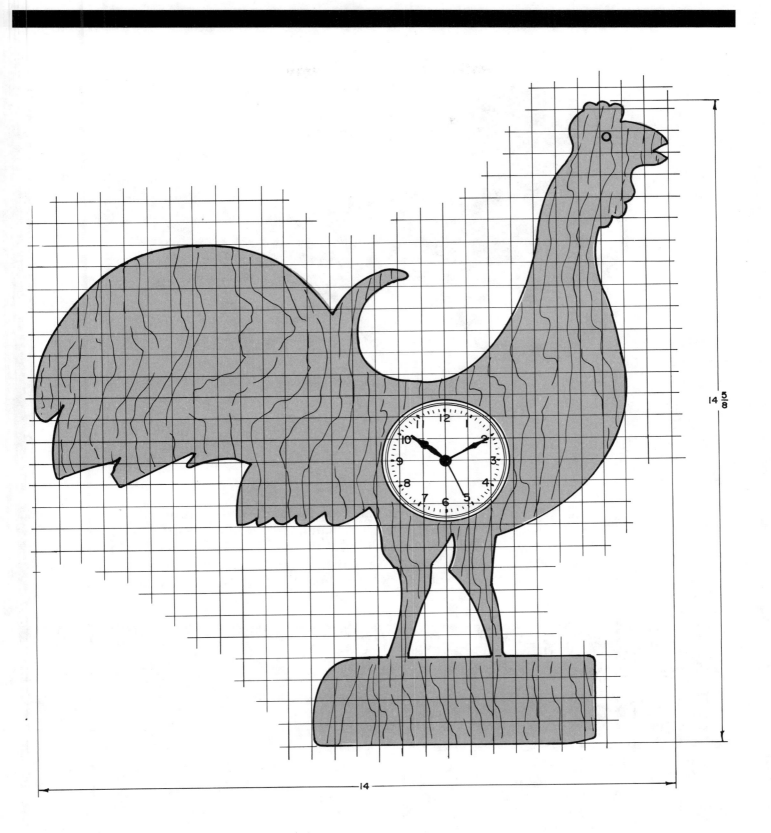

$14\frac{5}{8}$

14

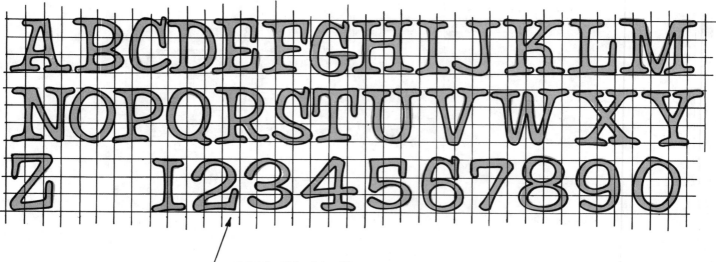

Mailbox sign: weather vane pattern No. 45, 6 by 10 inches, (a ½-inch grid was used). Cut the pattern from ½-inch hardwood. Patterns for letters and numbers are included in this book; use a photocopier or the grid method to enlarge or reduce them to an appropriate size. An exterior varnish over the entire project will protect it from the elements.

ABCDEFGHIJKLM
NOPQRSTUVWXY
Z 1234567890

— GRID TO SUIT

SIDE VIEW

Doorstop: weather vane pattern No. 52, 8¼ by 9 inches (a ⅝-inch grid was used). The pattern was cut from ¾-inch hardwood and painted dull black to make it look like a cast-iron doorstop.

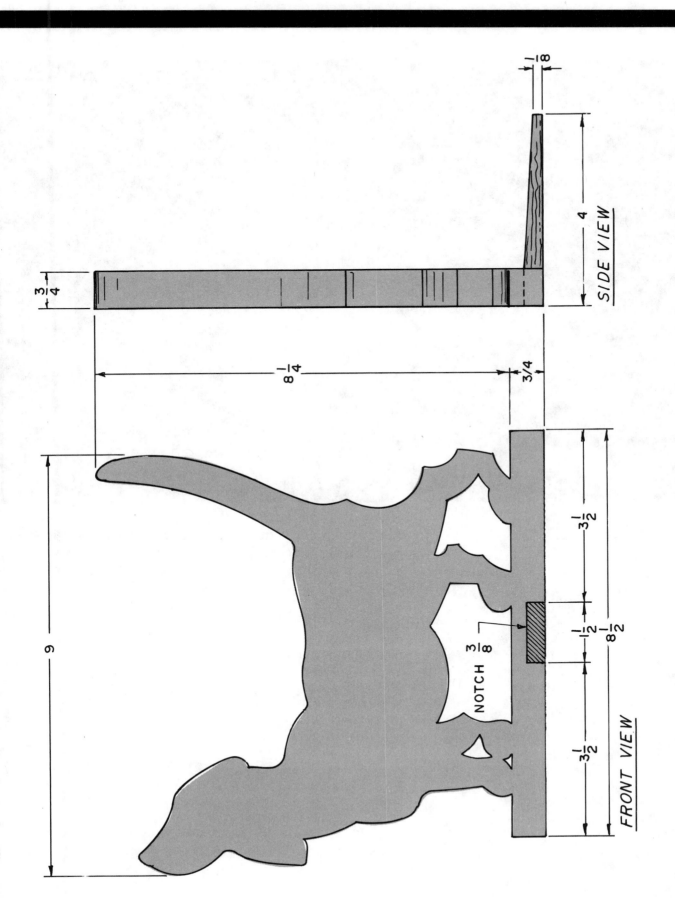

SIDE VIEW

FRONT VIEW

NOTCH $\frac{3}{8}$

Bookends: weather vane pattern No. 41, 6 by 6½ inches (a ½-inch grid was used). The two matching parts were cut out and sanded while taped together with double-faced masking tape to ensure that they would be symmetric.

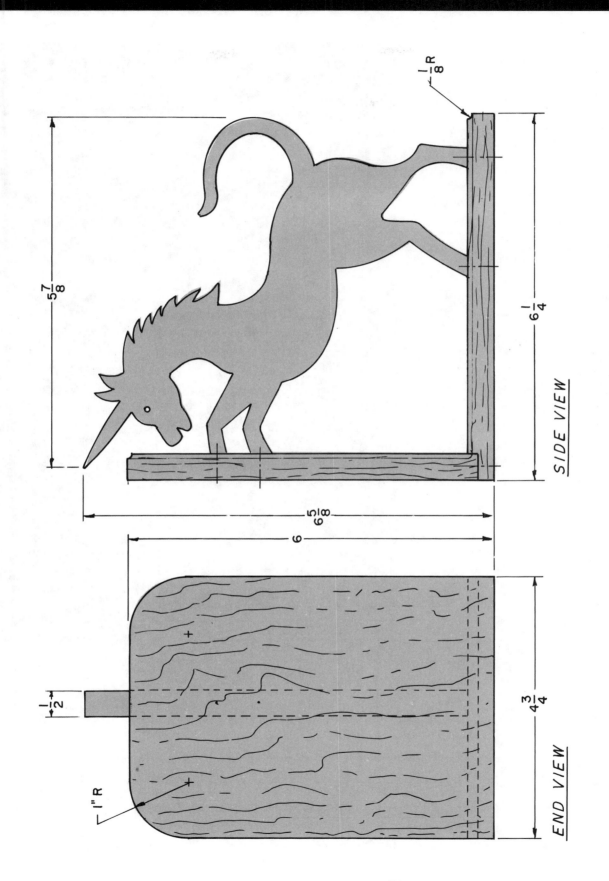

$\frac{1}{8}$R

$5\frac{7}{8}$

$6\frac{1}{4}$

$6\frac{5}{8}$

SIDE VIEW

6

$\frac{1}{2}$

1"R

$4\frac{3}{4}$

END VIEW

Welcome sign: weather vane pattern No. 8, 6½ by 8 inches (a ½-inch grid was used). It is held in place with ¼-inch-diameter dowels as shown. Apply a coat of exterior varnish for protection.

WELCOME

$\frac{1}{4}$ DOWEL

$8\frac{3}{8}$

$\frac{1}{2}$

$1\frac{3}{4}$

$1\frac{1}{8}$

$1\frac{1}{2}$

$1\frac{3}{4}$

13

$6\frac{1}{2}$

8

FRONT VIEW

$\frac{1}{4}$ GRID

SIDE VIEW

Signpost: weather vane pattern No. 37, 8½ by 11¼ inches (a ⁵/₁₆-inch grid was used). Use ⁵/₈-inch hardwood. Use a photocopier or the grid method to produce the desired size for the lettering.

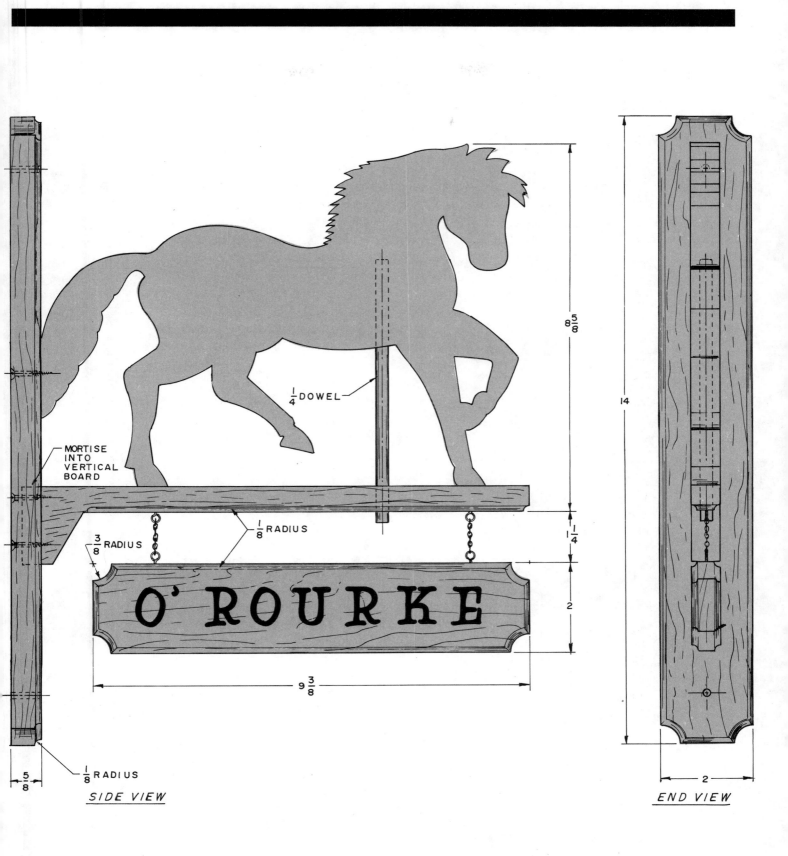

$8\frac{5}{8}$

$\frac{1}{4}$ DOWEL

14

MORTISE
INTO
VERTICAL
BOARD

$\frac{1}{8}$ RADIUS

$\frac{3}{8}$ RADIUS

$1\frac{1}{4}$

O' ROURKE

2

$9\frac{3}{8}$

$\frac{1}{8}$ RADIUS

$\frac{5}{8}$

SIDE VIEW

2

END VIEW

The Patterns

WEATHERCOCKS

The cock has been a Christian symbol since the ninth century, when by papal decree it became a symbol of the betrayal of Christ. Church officials were ordered to affix a cock at the peak of all church buildings. The cock reminded believers not to sin and to pray each morning. These early roof fixtures didn't indicate the weather, but as years passed some of them were converted into weather vanes.

The symbol gradually lost its religious significance, perhaps because the cock is also associated with the dawning of a new day. The rooster that greets the first sun makes a fitting choice for a weather vane motif.

The earliest rooster weather vane recorded in the United States is still in use atop the First Church in Albany, New York. It was brought here from Holland in 1656.

Aside from the simple arrow, the rooster has been the most popular theme ever used for a weather vane. This common motif is easily recognizable from a distance. Early weathercocks were two-dimensional and usually very plain. By 1850 or so, many were made of copper with three-dimensional bodies. With the Victorian era came the popularity of highly ornamented houses, and the weathercock was replaced by more modern motifs.

The New England countryside today still has many original rooster weather vanes dating back to the 1700s. Considering their popularity, it is surprising that very few original rooster weather vanes can be found outside of New England, New York, and Pennsylvania.

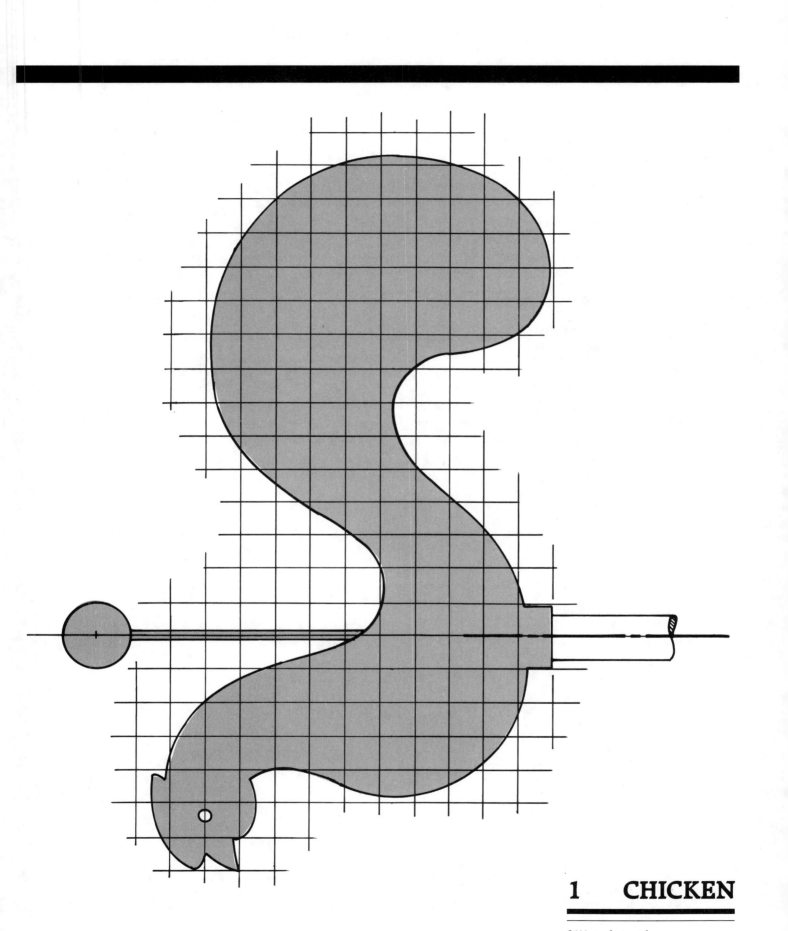

1 CHICKEN

21½ inches wide

2 CHICKEN

13 inches wide

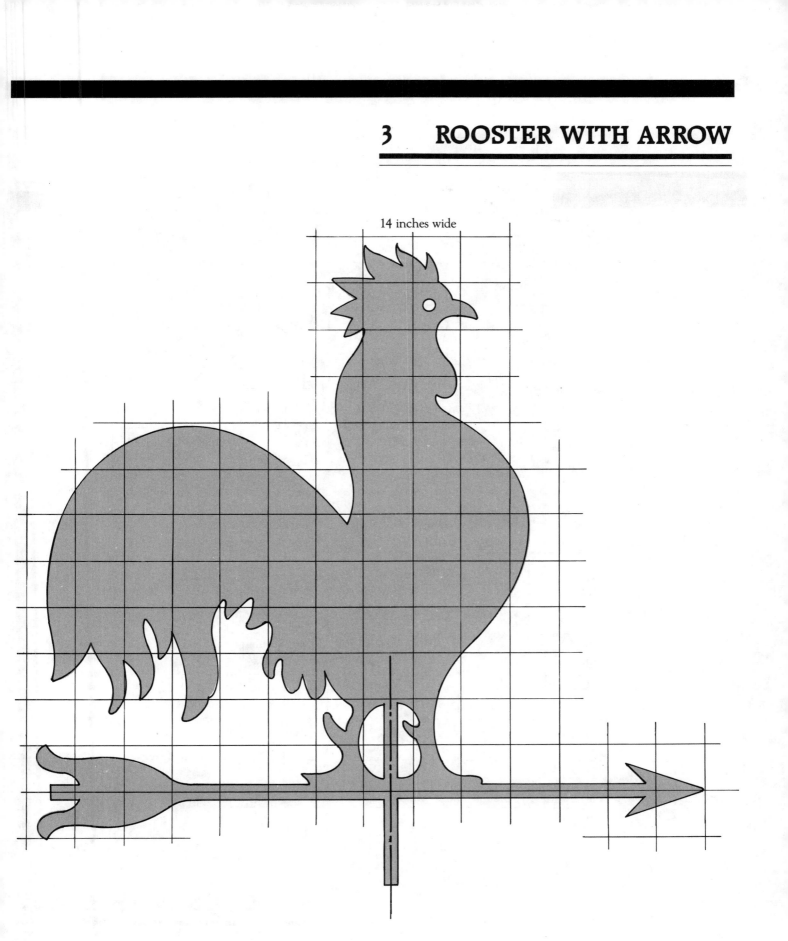

14 inches wide

4 COCK WITH ARROW

16 inches wide

5 ROOSTER WITH ARROW

c. 1865
zinc
26 inches wide

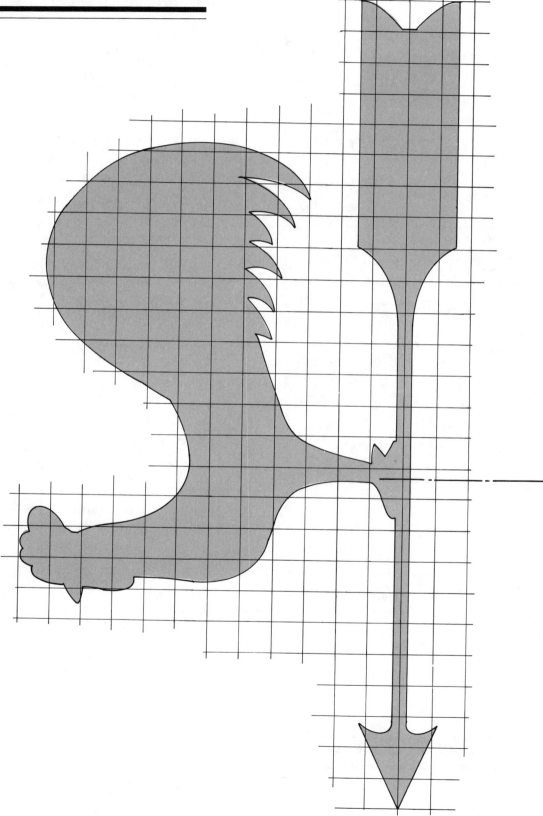

6   CROWING COCK

c. 1919
15 inches wide

7 **EARLY ROOSTER**

c. 1763
15 inches wide

8 ROOSTER

15½ inches wide

DOWEL 7/16" DIA.

9   ROOSTER

c. 1880
wood
found in Bridgeton, Maine
20 inches wide

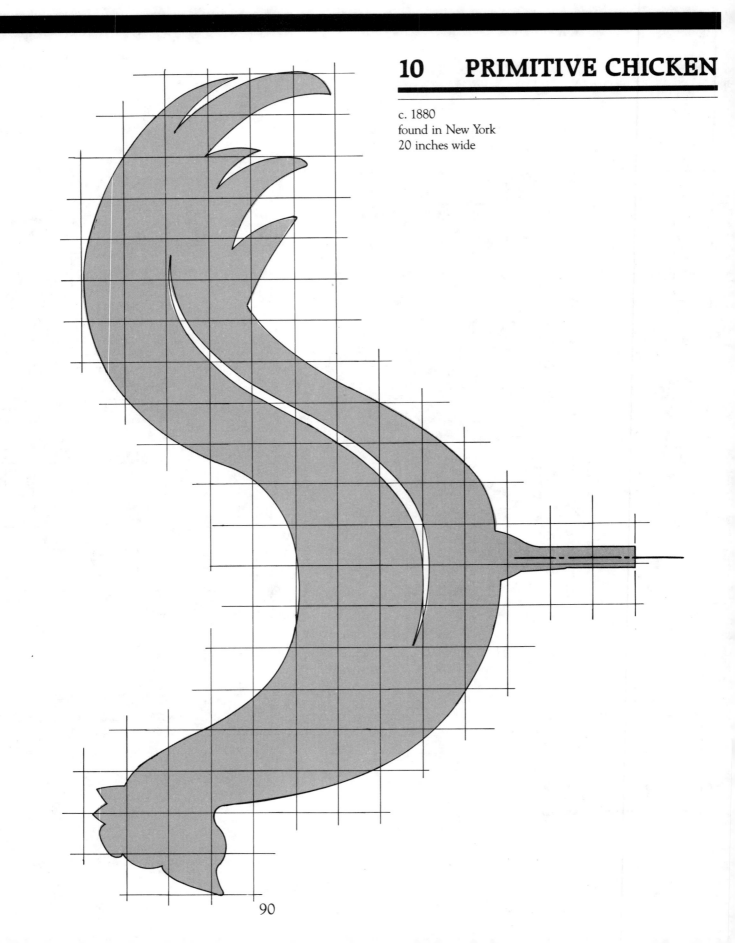

c. 1880
found in New York
20 inches wide

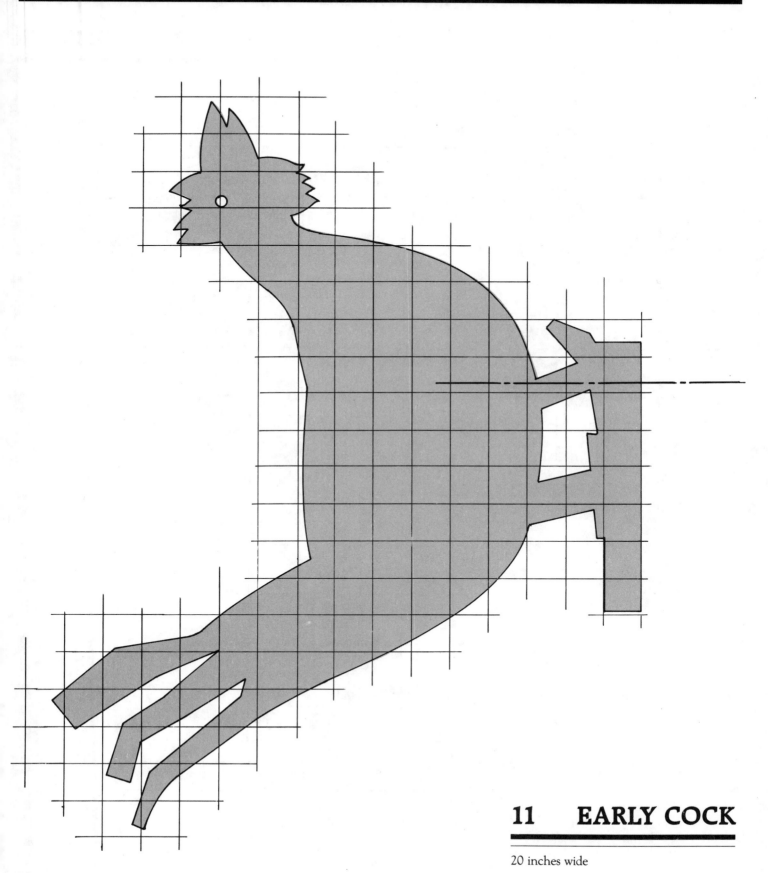

11   EARLY COCK

20 inches wide

13   ROOSTER

12 inches wide

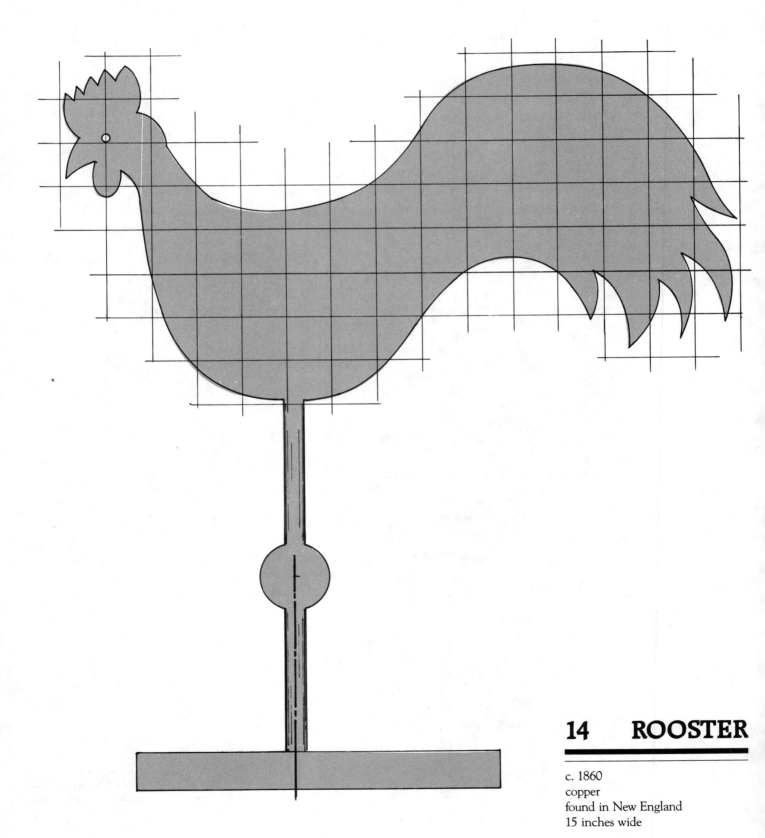

14   ROOSTER

c. 1860
copper
found in New England
15 inches wide

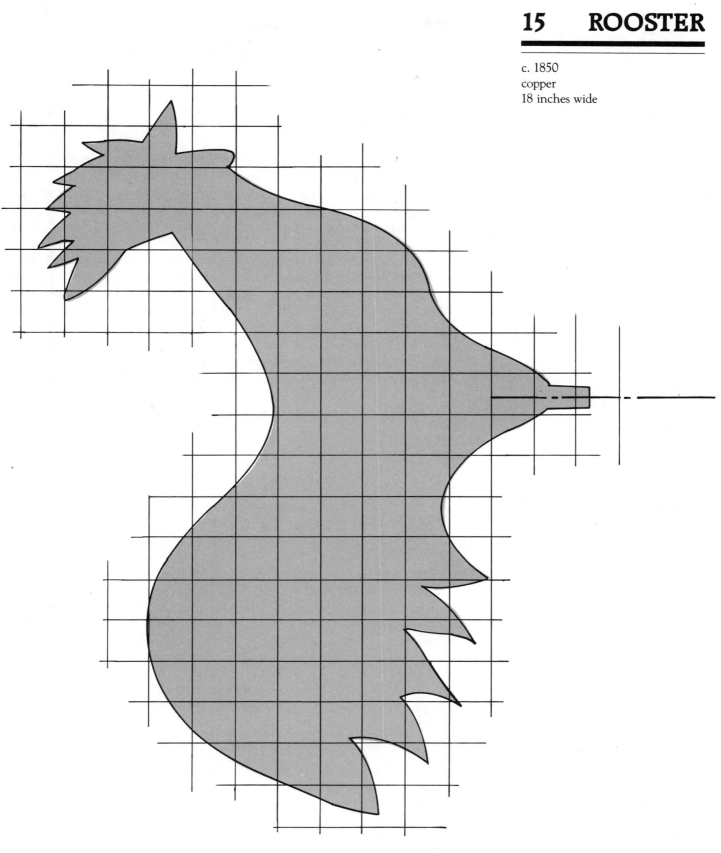

c. 1850
copper
18 inches wide

FISHES AND WHALES

In collecting photographs, drawings, and catalogs of weather vanes over the years, I have been amazed to find so many fish patterns. Fish motifs are nearly as popular as roosters and may even surpass farm animal motifs. New England's proximity to the Atlantic Ocean may explain this enthusiasm for fish vanes. Early New Englanders earned much of their livelihood from the sea, and knowing which way the wind blew must have been especially important to their survival. Their ties to the sea made the choice of fish and whale motifs quite fitting. The use of the fish as a Christian symbol may also have contributed to its popularity as a weather vane motif.

Like the rooster, the fish makes an excellent indicator. It is easily identifiable and it balances well. In addition, the fish shape appears to withstand weathering better than most other motifs because of its simple lines. Many original wooden fish weather vanes remain in use in the very locations where they were first placed.

The whale, cod, trout, and swordfish seem to have been the most popular designs, although dolphins and sea horses were also used by seacoast inhabitants. Included in the following collection of weather vane patterns are a sea serpent and a mermaid.

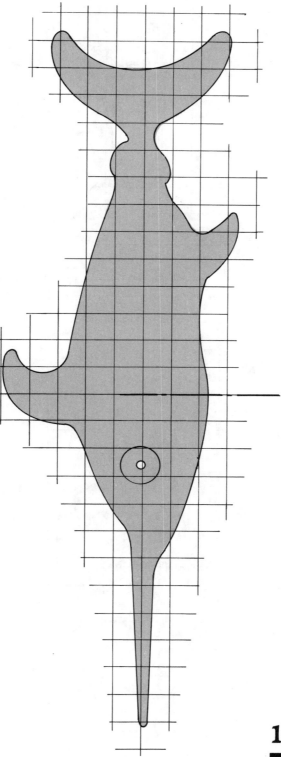

16   SWORDFISH

26 inches long

17   CODFISH

c. 1900
carved wood
29½ inches long

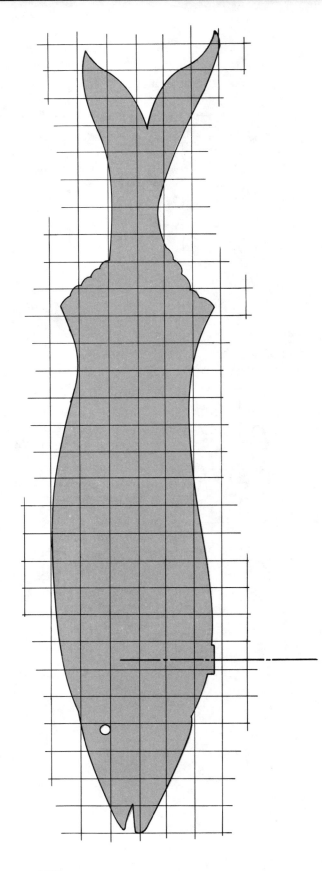

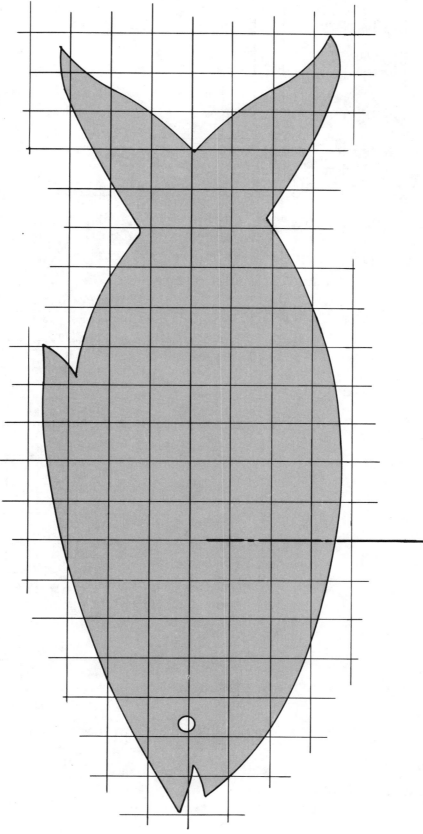

18   FISH

20 inches long

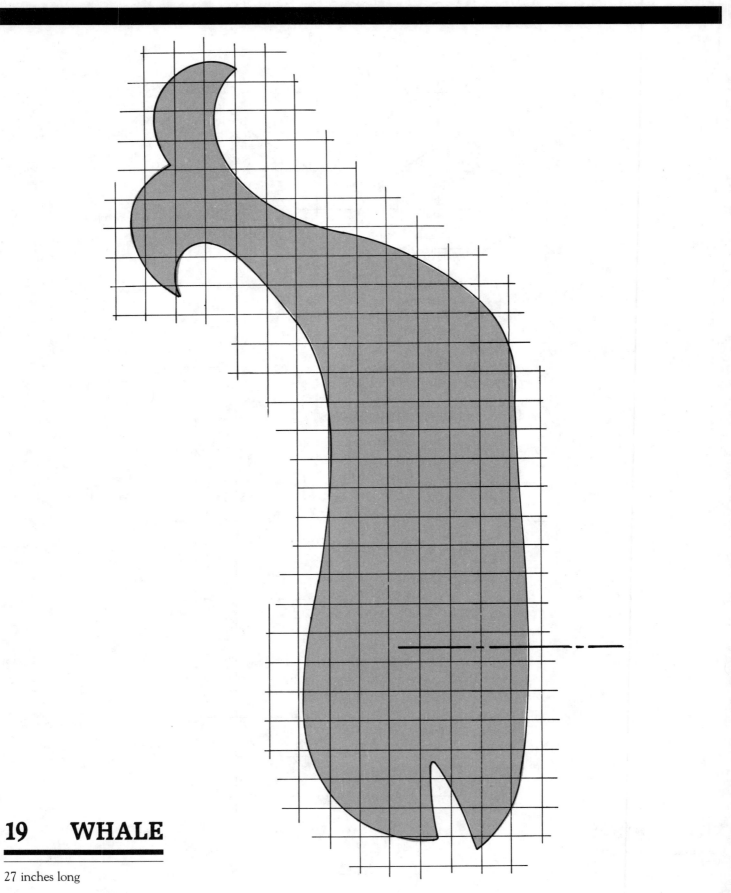

19 WHALE

27 inches long

20 BROOK TROUT

c. 1825
wood
28¾ inches long

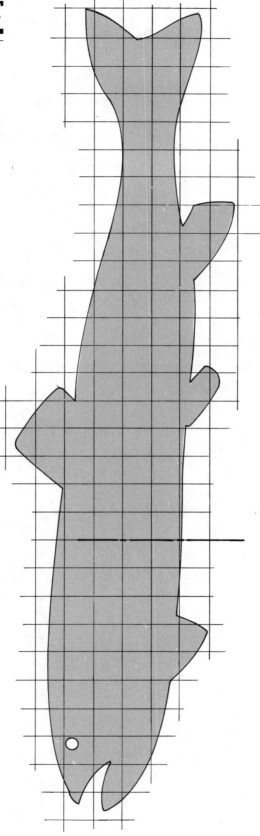

21   CODFISH

c. 1880
27 inches long

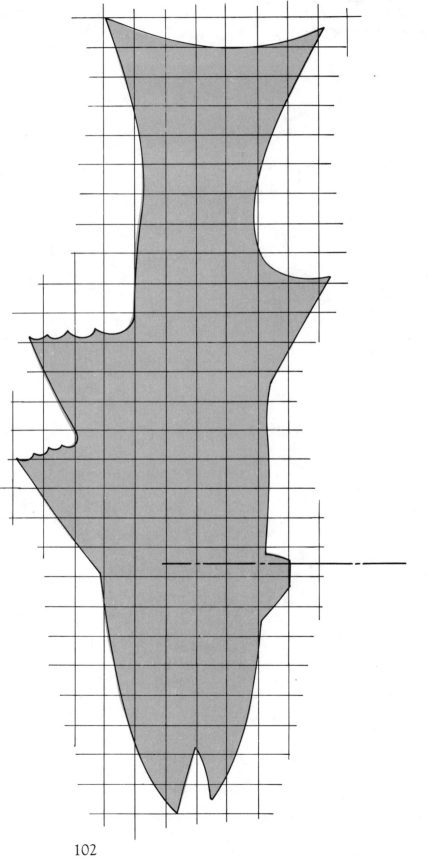

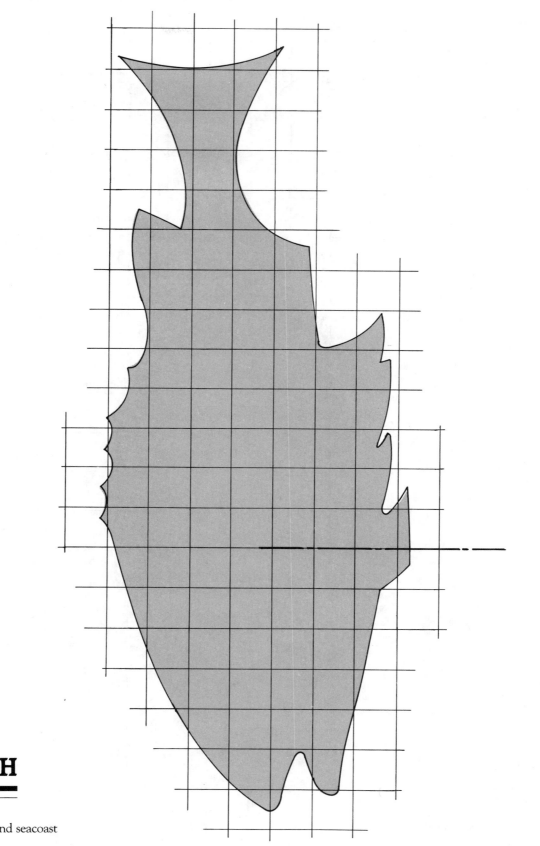

22　FISH

c. 1860
found on New England seacoast
19 inches long

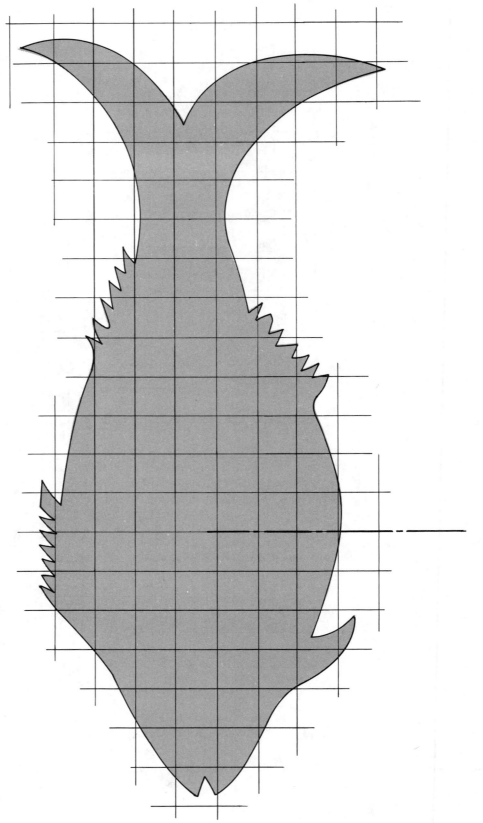

23 FISH

c. 1880
found in Millersville, Pennsylvania
20 inches long

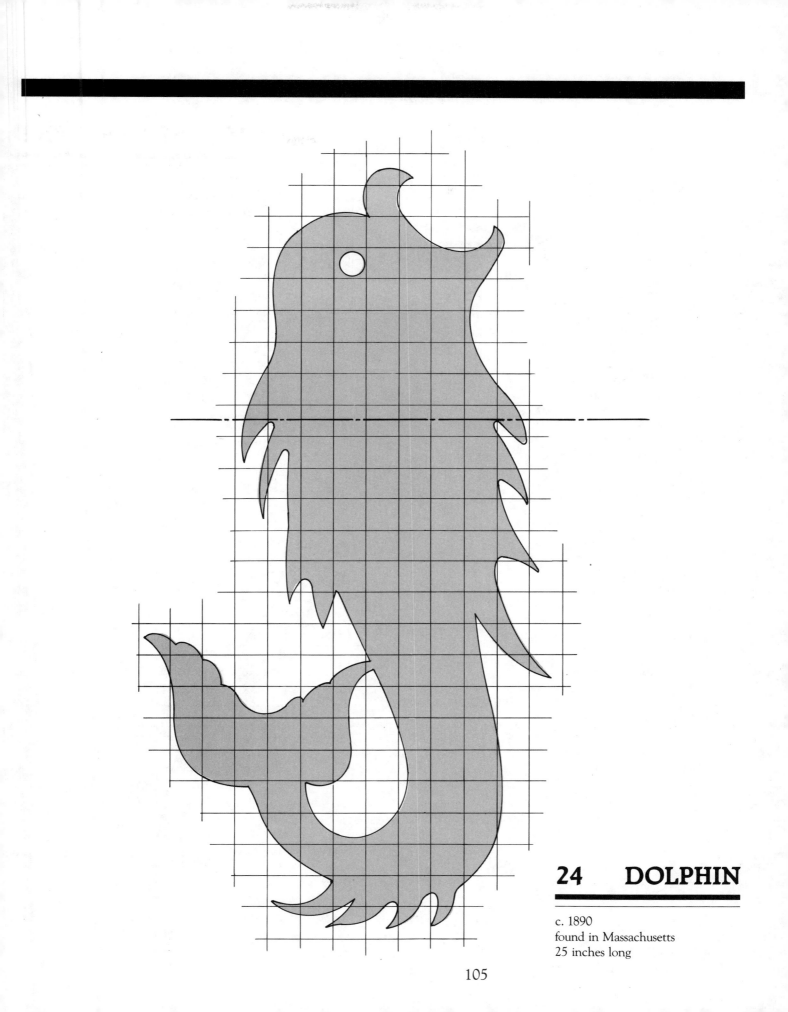

24   DOLPHIN

c. 1890
found in Massachusetts
25 inches long

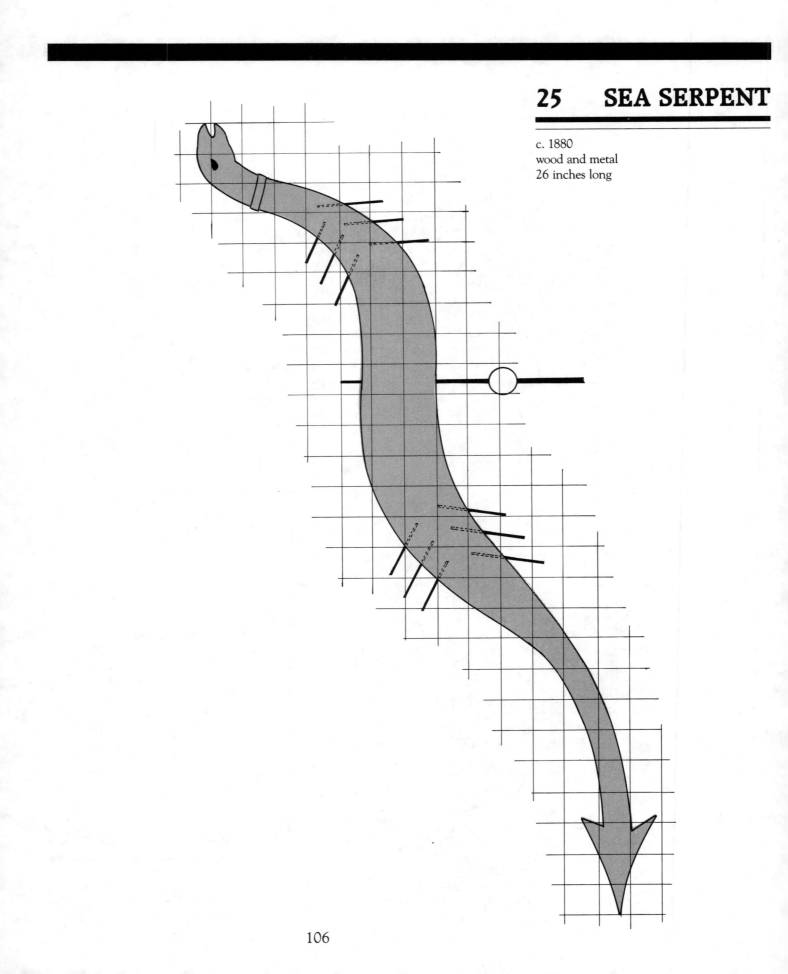

c. 1880
wood and metal
26 inches long

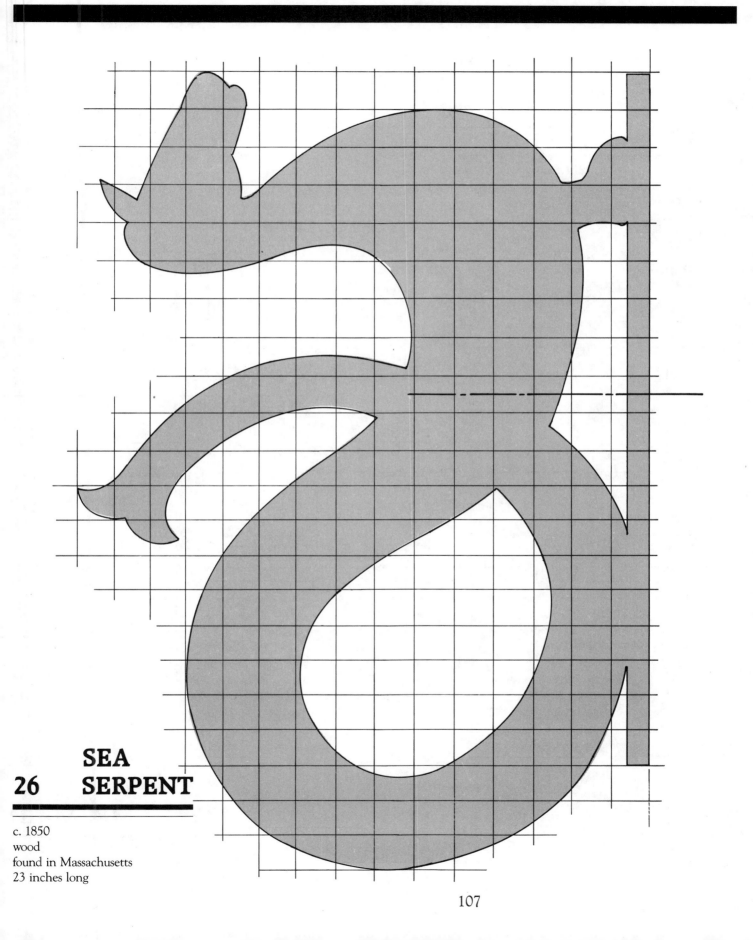

26 SEA SERPENT

c. 1850
wood
found in Massachusetts
23 inches long

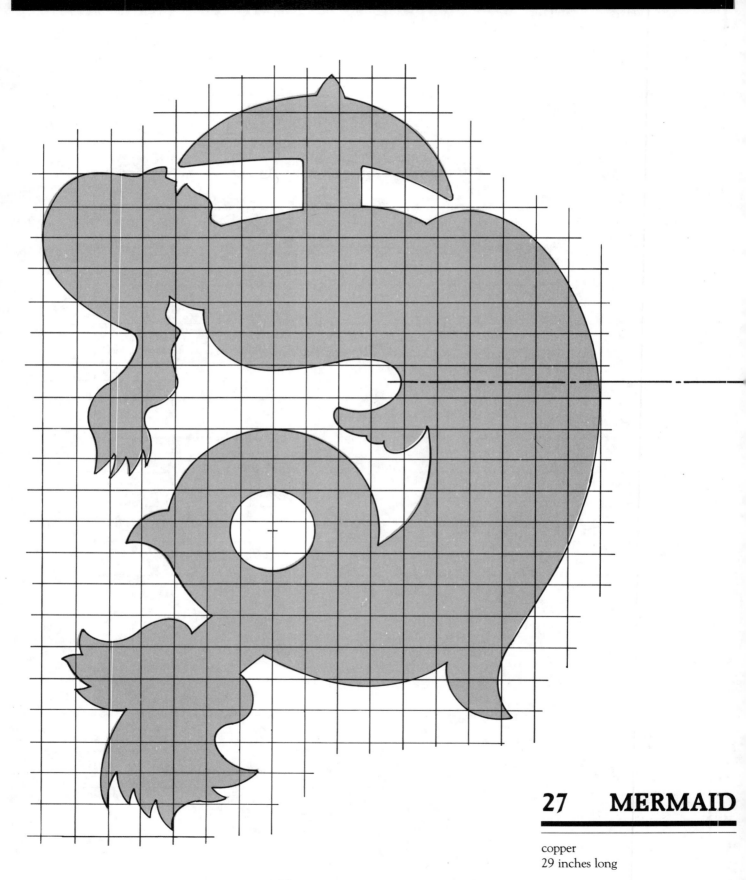

27 **MERMAID**

copper
29 inches long

28   TRITON, GOD OF THE SEA

c. 1810
32 inches long

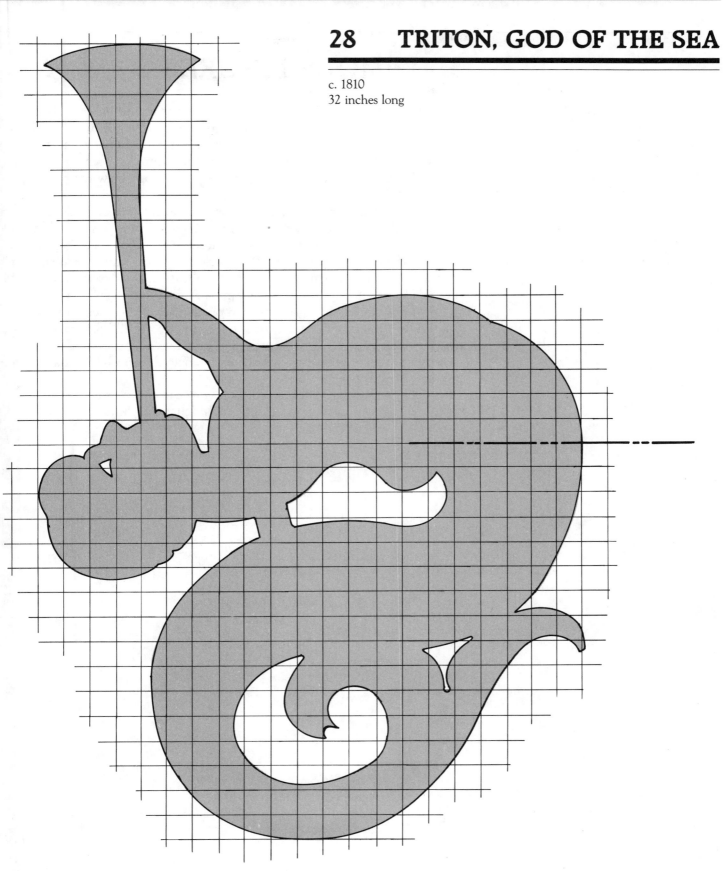

RELIGIOUS FIGURES

These charming early weather vanes were especially primitive. The designers of these motifs did not have the luxury of referring to real-life objects when drawing these winged angelic figures. Many designs were crude and out of proportion. Some were thin, some fat, some masculine, some feminine, some clothed, and some nude. Many blew trumpets in praise of God.

Angel Gabriel, an especially popular subject, was crafted in all shapes and sizes. One very famous Angel Gabriel came from the Universalist Church in Newburyport, Massachusetts. Made in approximately 1840 by the company of Gould and Hazlett of Charlestown, it is six feet two inches long and thirty-four inches high. Its crafters used thirty-eight pounds' worth of $1/16$-inch gilded copper. After the church burned in 1888, the weather vane was mounted on the nearby Peoples United Methodist Church, where it stands today. In 1965 the U.S. Postal Service used its likeness on a large printing of Christmas stamps. After the stamp was issued, people noticed that the male Angel Gabriel had female breasts. This discovery caused quite a stir.

The following patterns are as close to the originals as possible—authentically out of proportion, but each delightful in its own way.

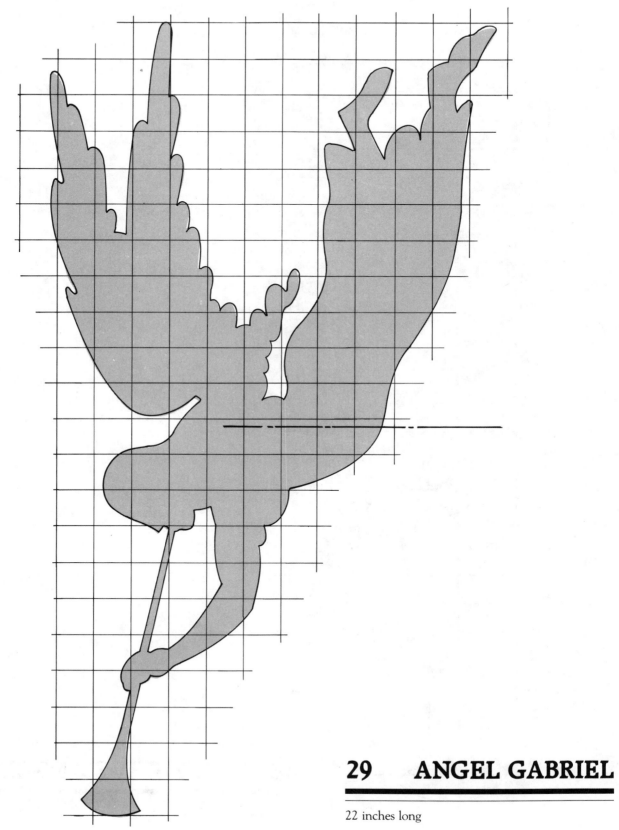

29   ANGEL GABRIEL

22 inches long

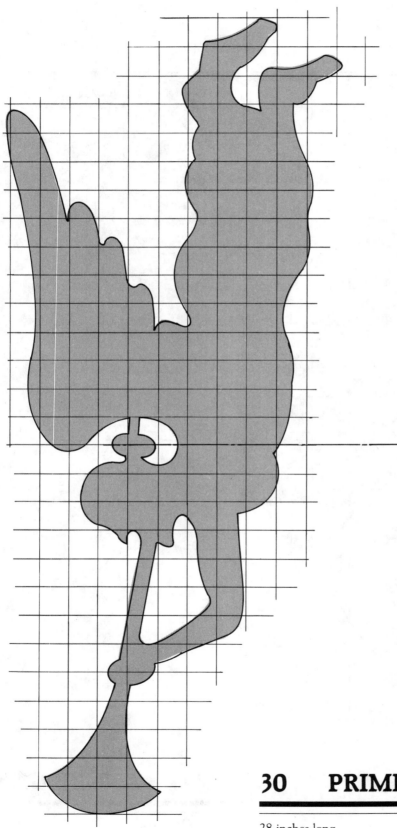

30 PRIMITIVE ANGEL GABRIEL

28 inches long

31   ANGEL

wood
26 inches long

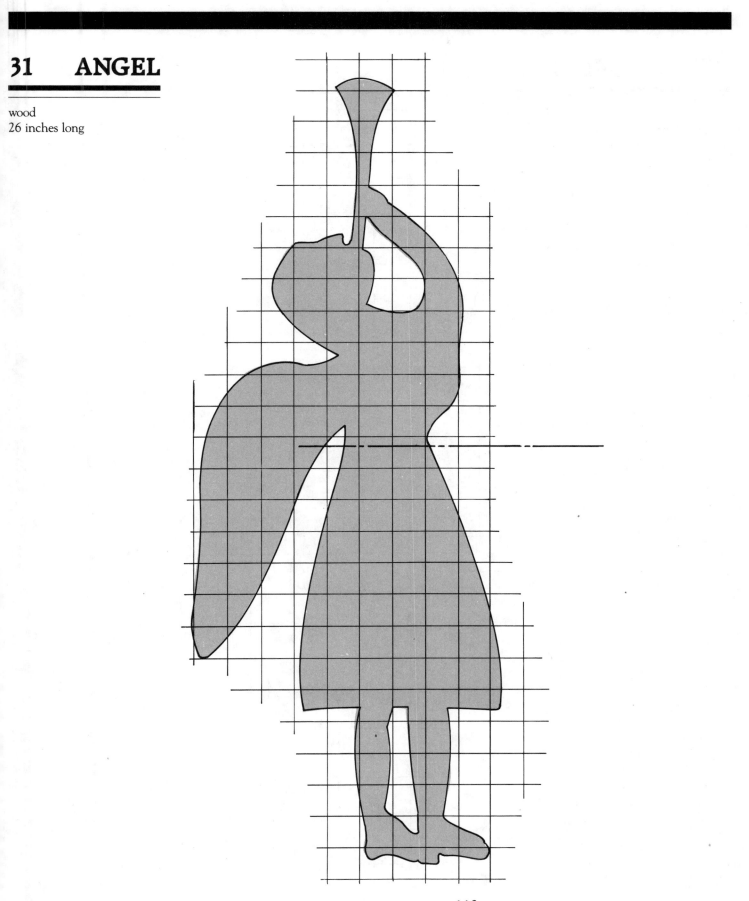

32   ANGEL GABRIEL

c. 1880
47 inches long

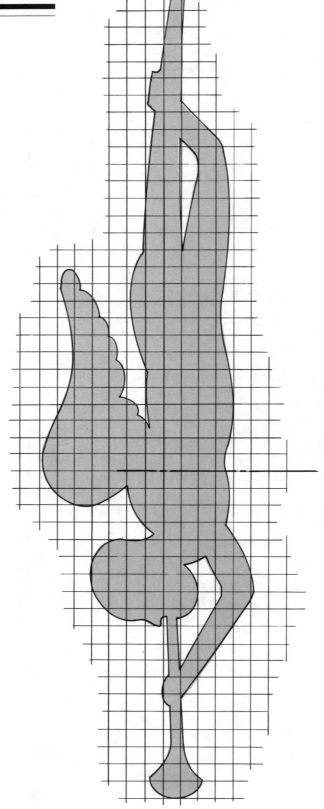

33   ANGEL GABRIEL

22 inches long

MAN WITH HORN

c. 1840
wood
found in Hudson, New York
40 inches long

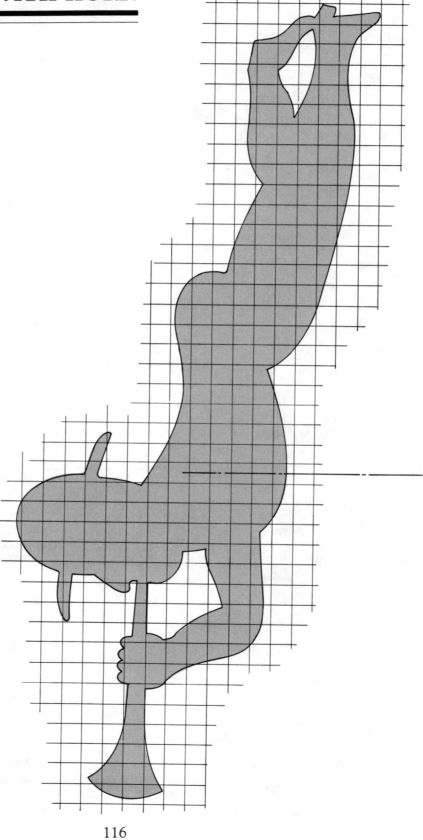

c. 1860
wood
found in Bucks County, Pennsylvania

35   HEX DOCTOR

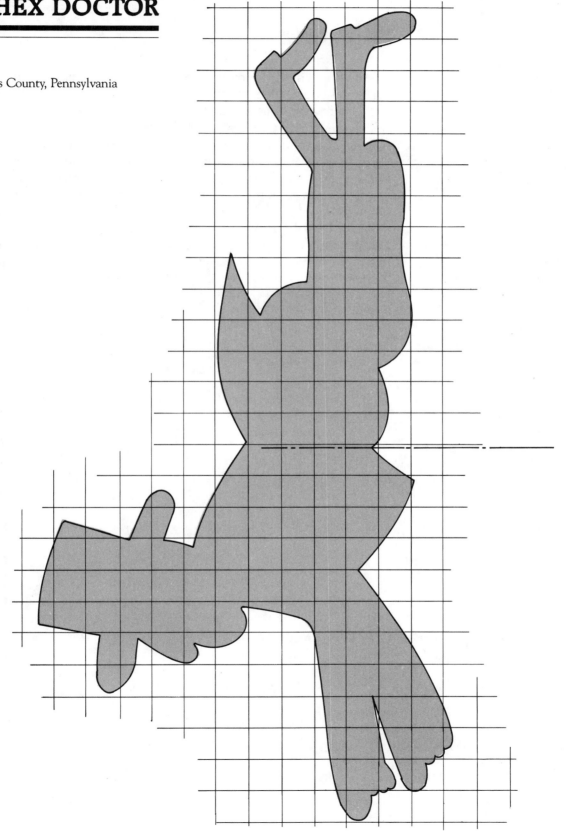

HORSES

The graceful silhouette of a spirited horse trotting along with a flowing tail makes an excellent motif. Throughout the years horses have proudly stood guard over houses and barns, where they surveyed meadows and fields, swinging at the pleasure of the wind.

Their popularity may be explained by the fact that the horse provided transportation and recreation, as well as economic support for many. Many early horse weather vanes portrayed famous racehorses of the day, usually running at a full gallop. Others were styled after the famous Currier and Ives prints.

In the 1920s and 1930s, the automobile replaced the horse as a weather vane motif, just as it replaced the horse as a mode of transportation. In due time horse weather vanes returned to favor, perhaps because the automobile had lost its novelty.

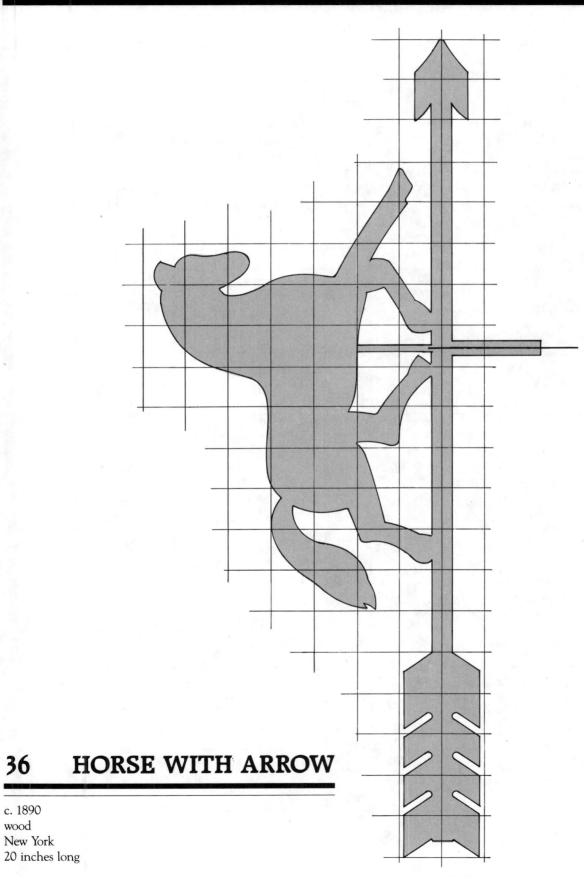

36 HORSE WITH ARROW

c. 1890
wood
New York
20 inches long

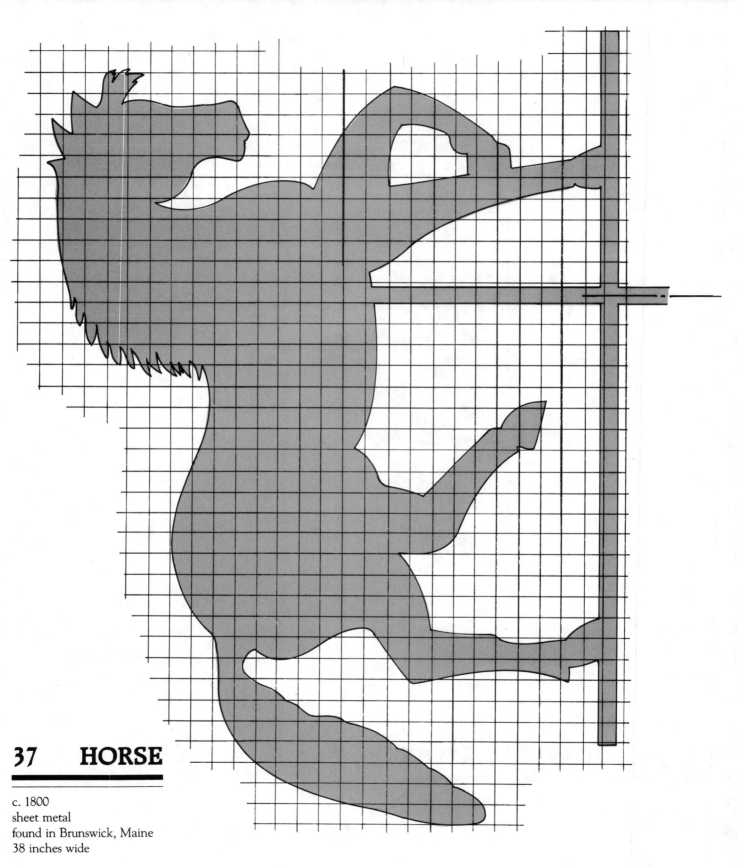

37 HORSE

c. 1800
sheet metal
found in Brunswick, Maine
38 inches wide

38 HORSE

20 inches wide

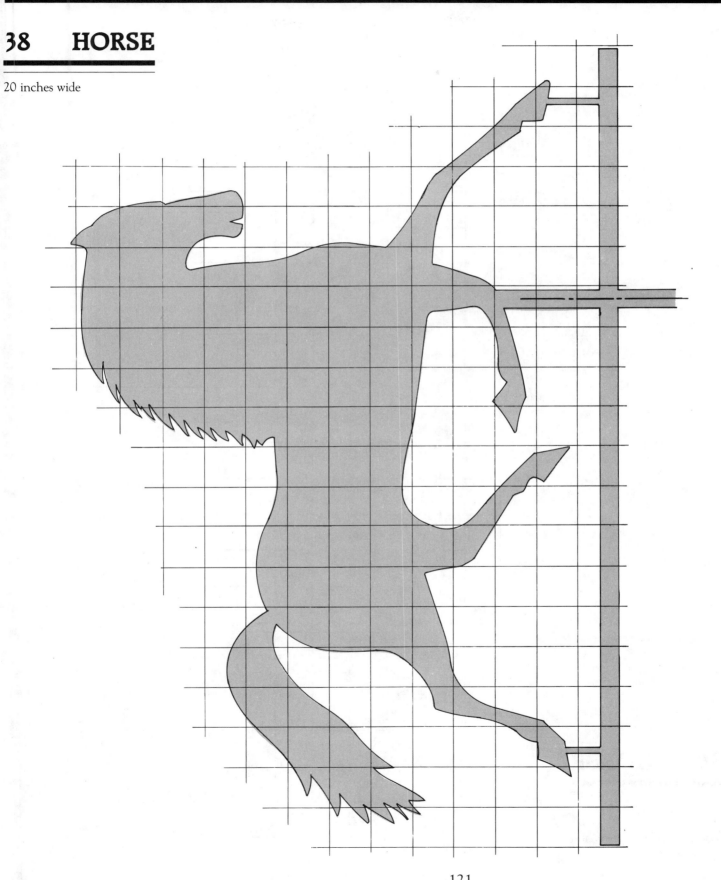

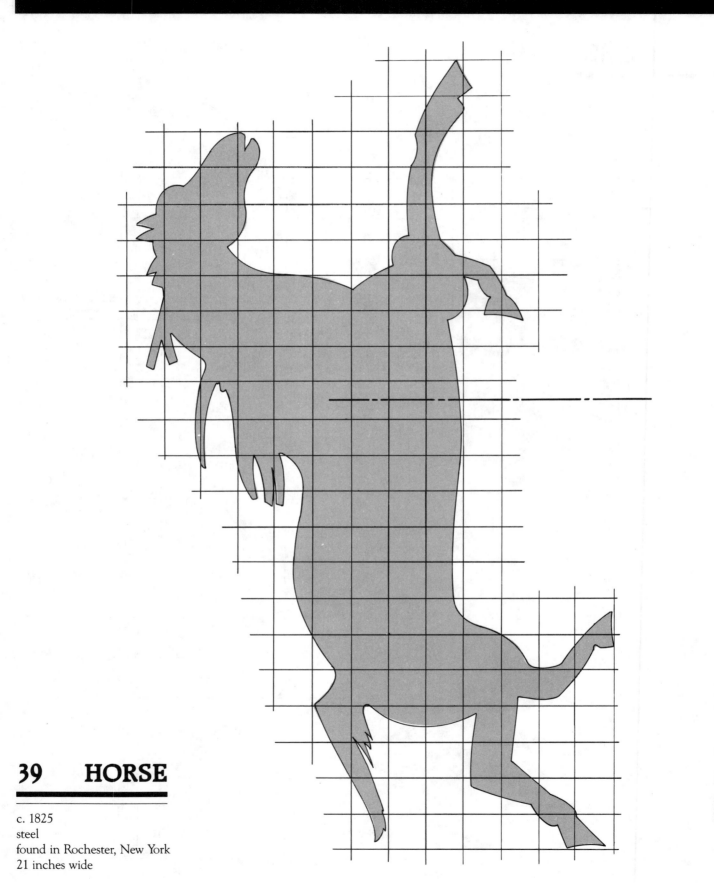

39   HORSE

c. 1825
steel
found in Rochester, New York
21 inches wide

40   PEGASUS, A WINGED HORSE

c. 1810
sheet iron
35 inches wide

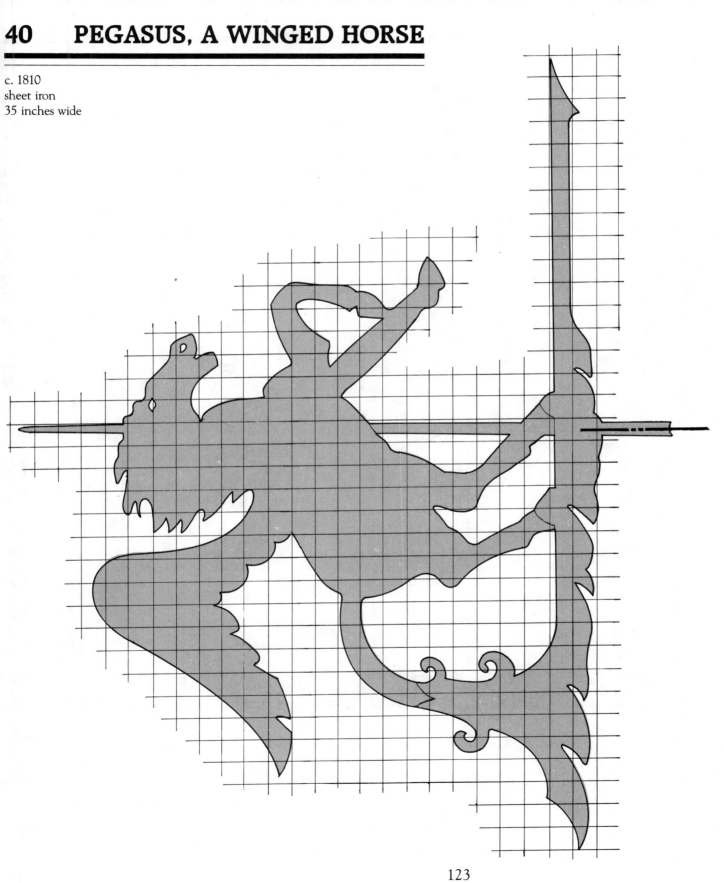

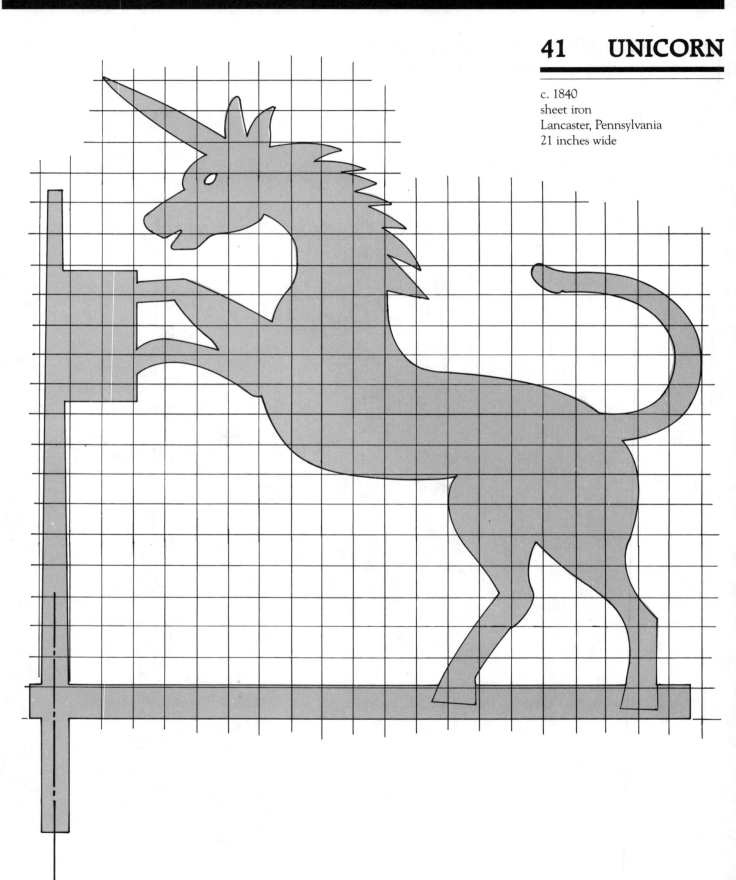

c. 1840
sheet iron
Lancaster, Pennsylvania
21 inches wide

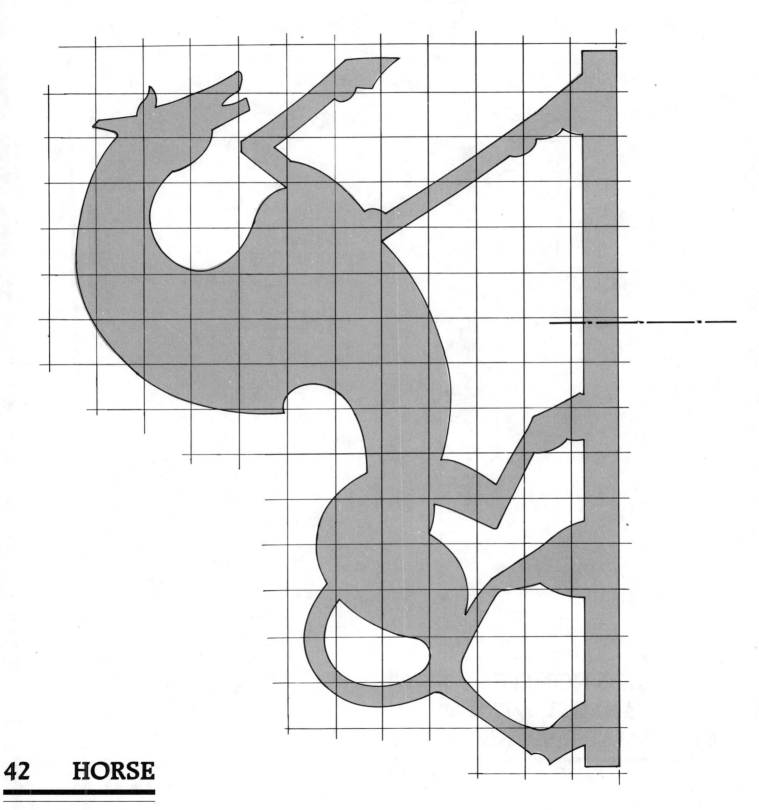

42 HORSE

16 inches wide

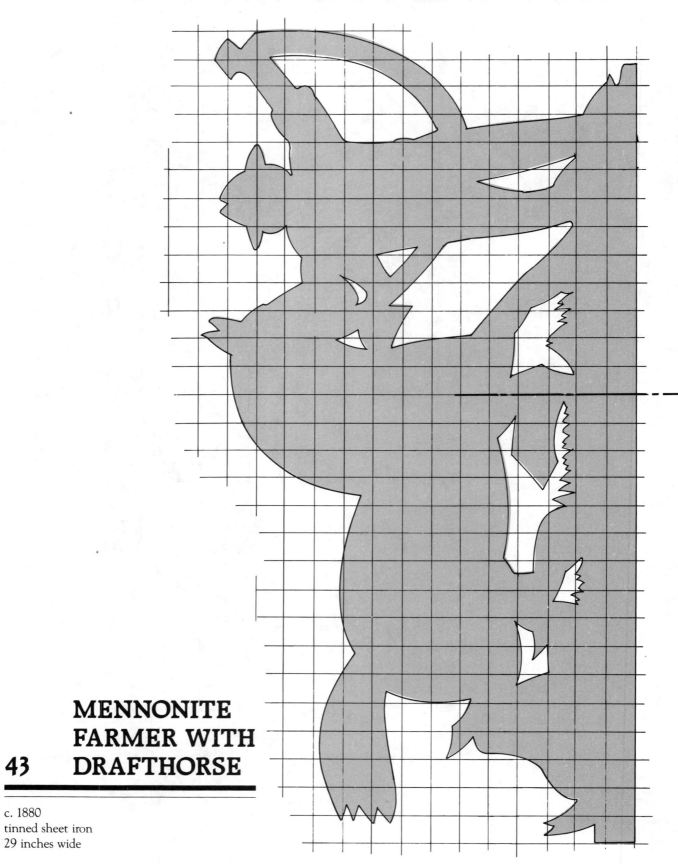

MENNONITE FARMER WITH DRAFTHORSE

43

c. 1880
tinned sheet iron
29 inches wide

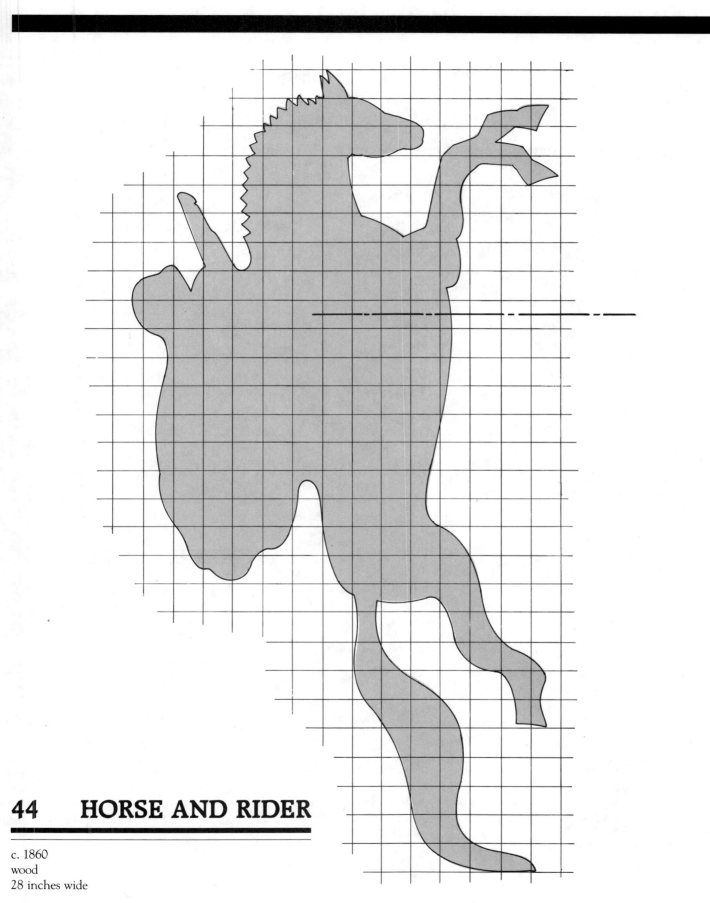

44   HORSE AND RIDER

c. 1860
wood
28 inches wide

**HORSE
AND
WAGON**

45

c. 1830
bronze

BARNYARD ANIMALS

Animals commonly found in barnyards—bulls, cows, pigs, sheep, dogs, even snakes—have all been motifs for weather vanes. These weather vanes were actually advertisements for a farm and its products. The choice often reflected a farmer's specialty, and sometimes his favorite animal. By 1850 or so, when farm animals had become popular as motifs, most weather vanes were made commercially. Consequently, they were often full bodied and made of copper, crafted in great numbers from specially made molds. Many of these barnyard animal weather vanes were large and elaborate.

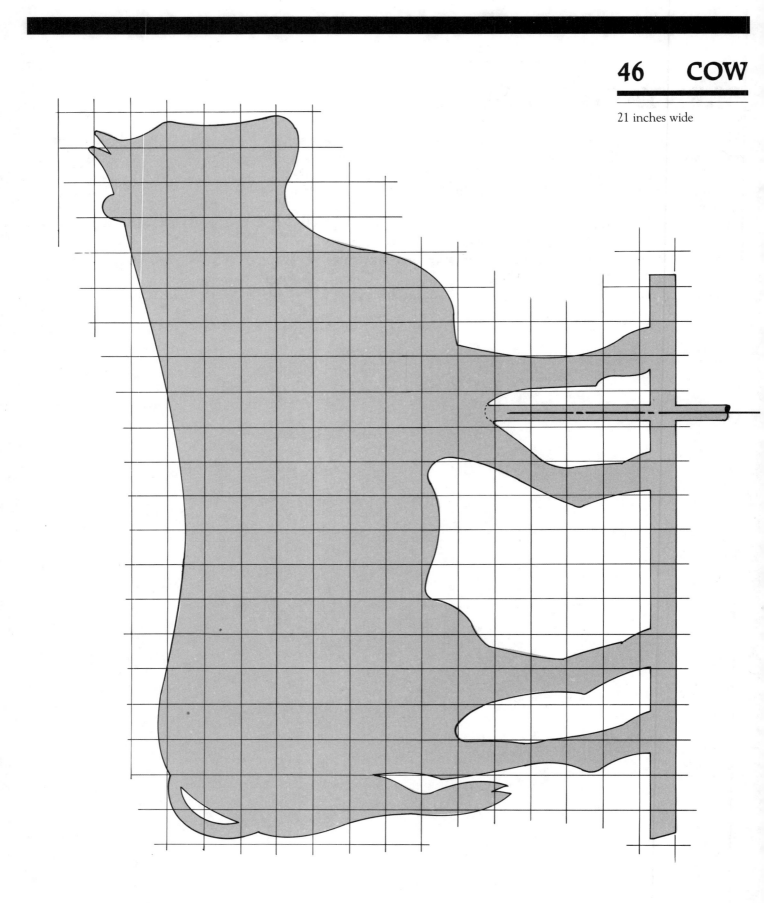

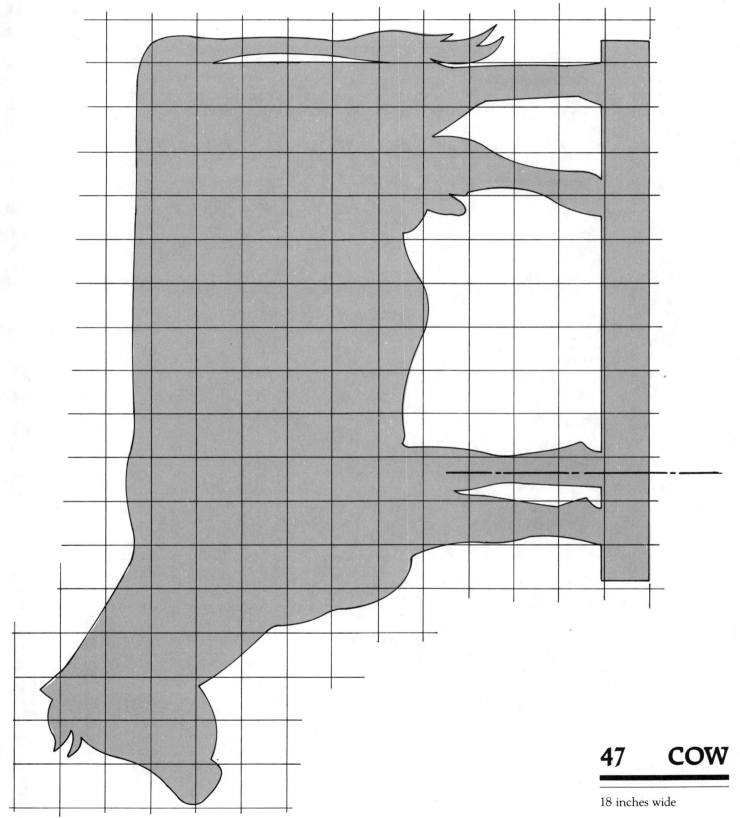

47 COW

18 inches wide

17 inches wide

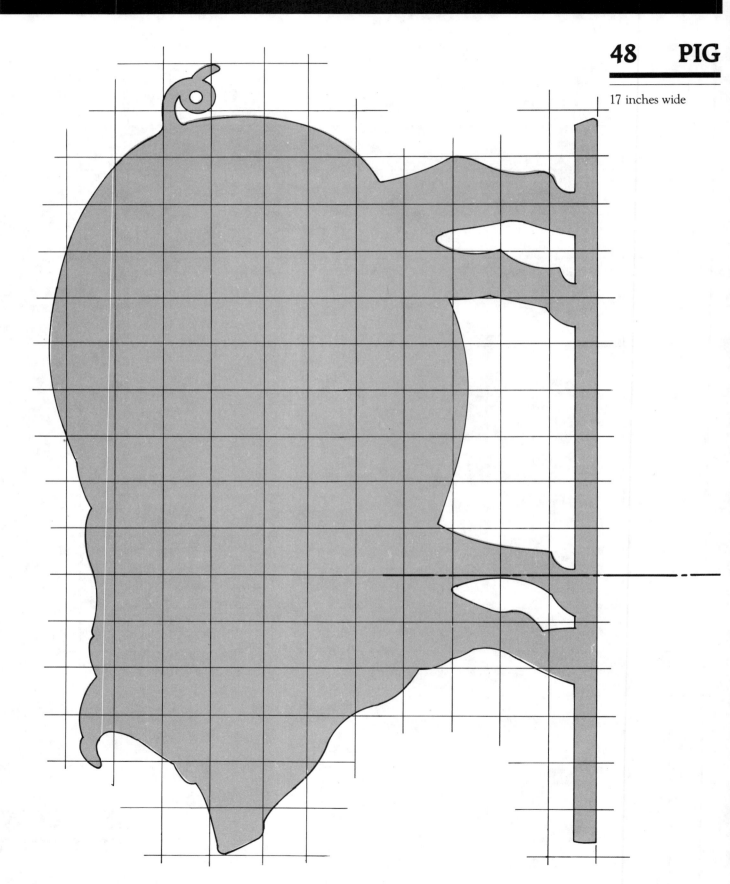

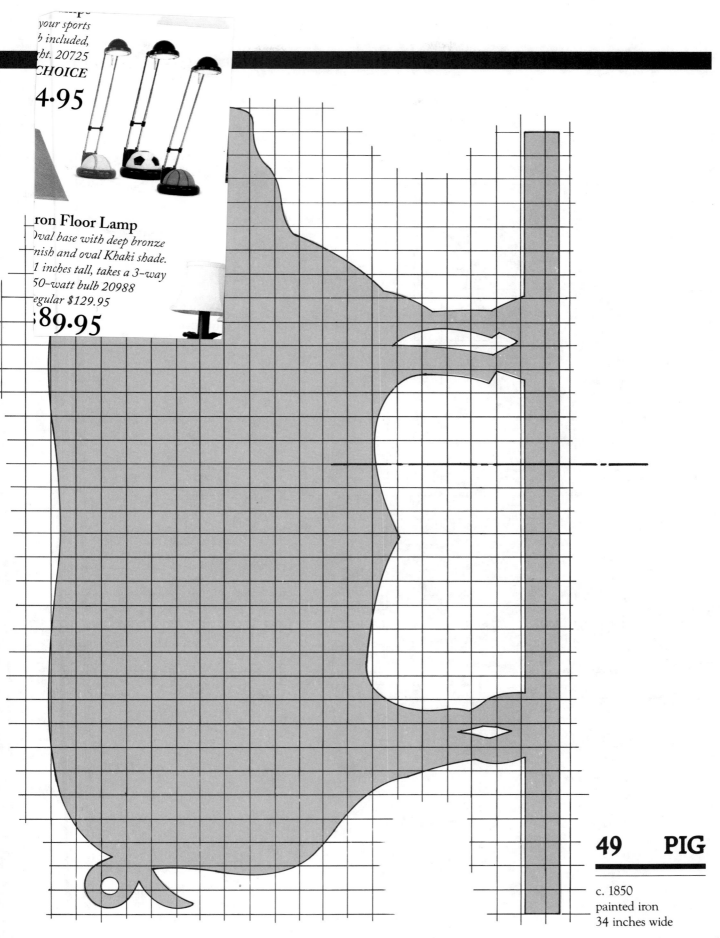

49   PIG

c. 1850
painted iron
34 inches wide

c. 1880
copper with gold leaf
made by A. B. and W. T. Westervelt
50 inches wide

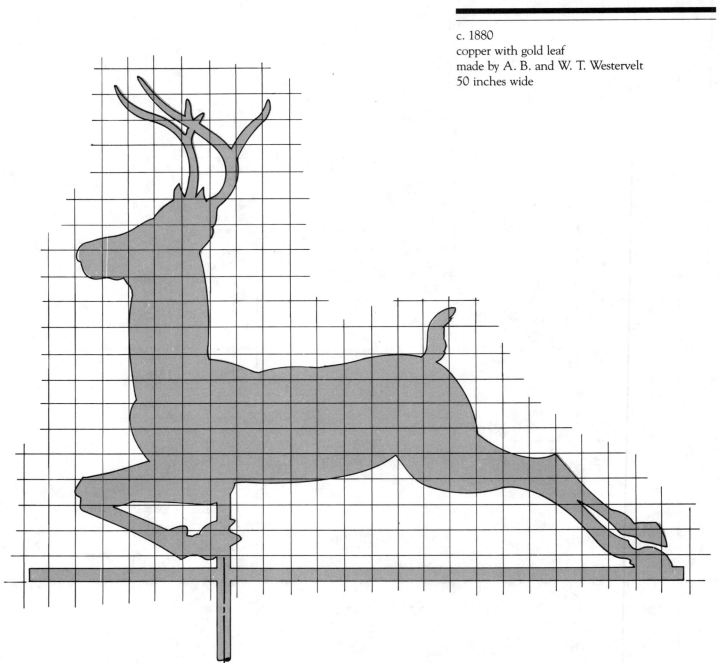

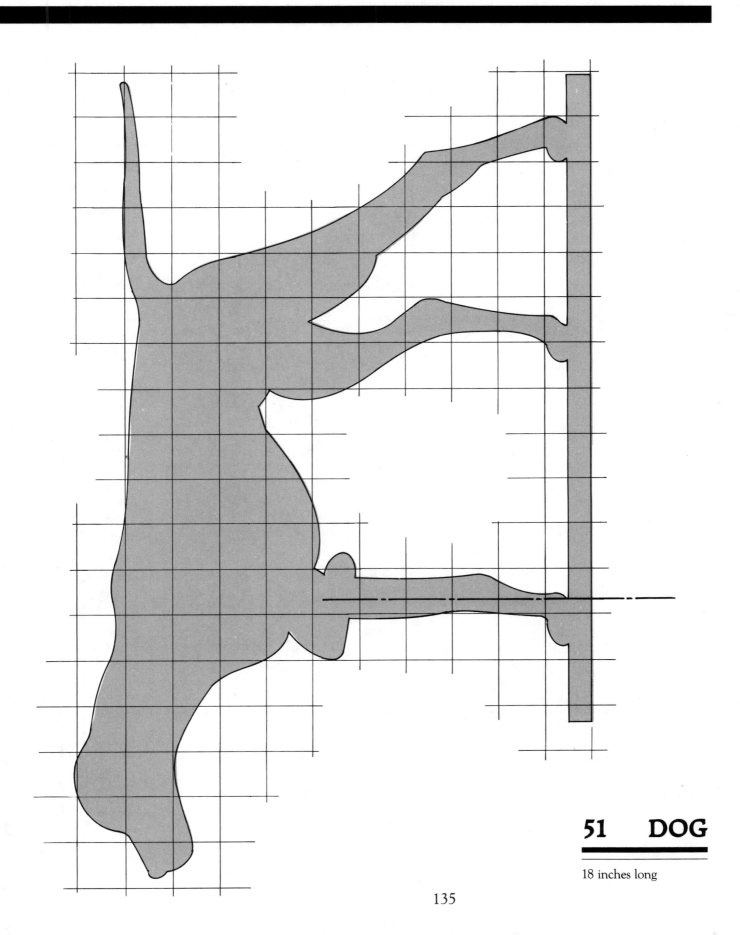

51 DOG

18 inches long

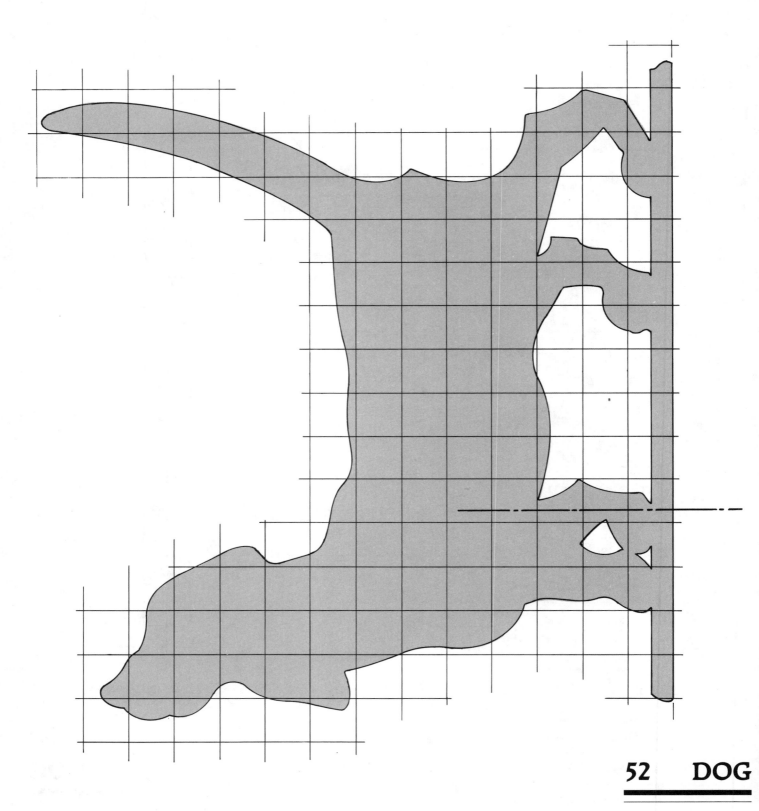

52 DOG

15 inches long

53   COILED SNAKE

1976
painted wood
made by Marshall Stone
36 inches wide

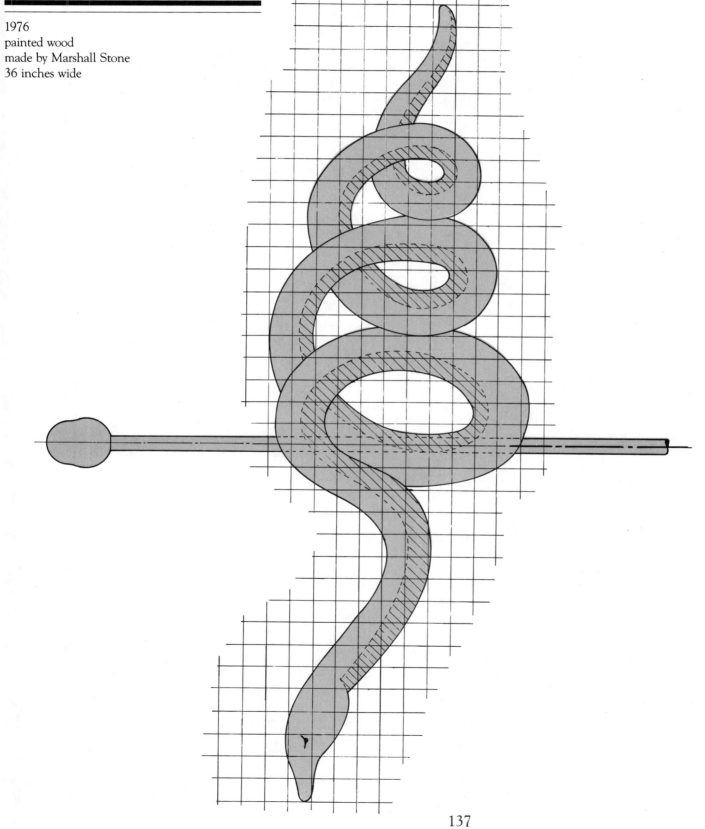

BIRDS

Birds other than roosters were often used for weather vanes. Among them were peacocks, doves, and wild birds, such as curlews. Eagle and owl weather vanes were especially popular. The eagle, our national symbol, depicted strength. The owl symbolized intelligence and wisdom.

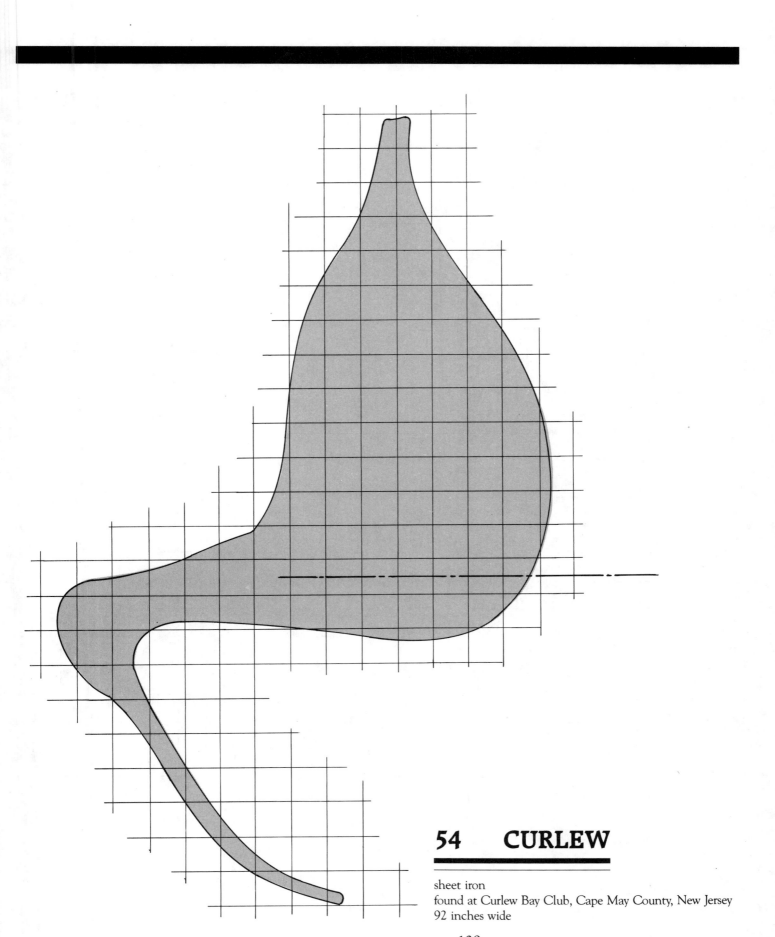

54   CURLEW

sheet iron
found at Curlew Bay Club, Cape May County, New Jersey
92 inches wide

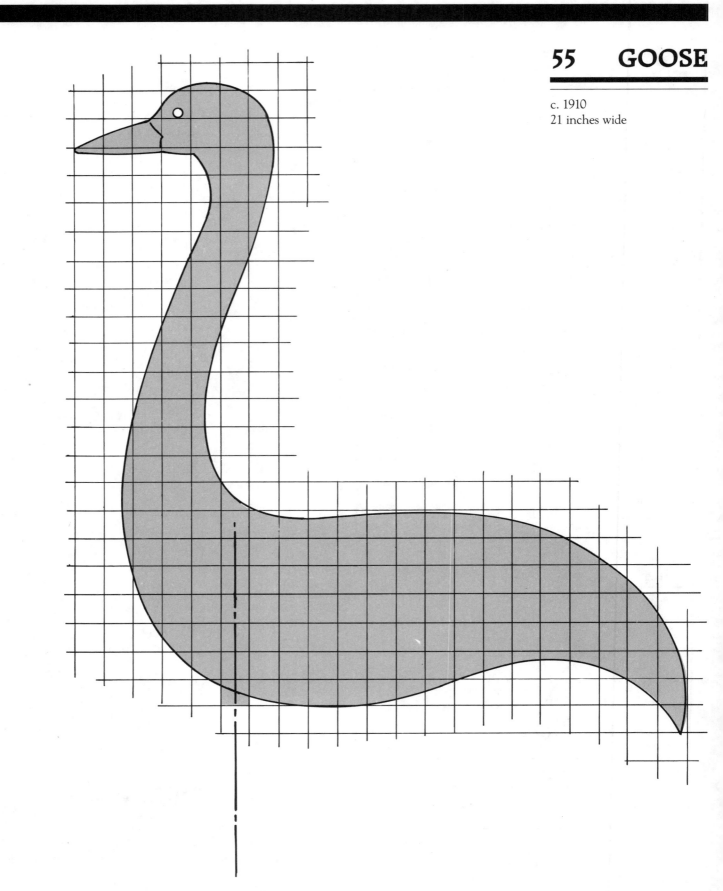

c. 1910
21 inches wide

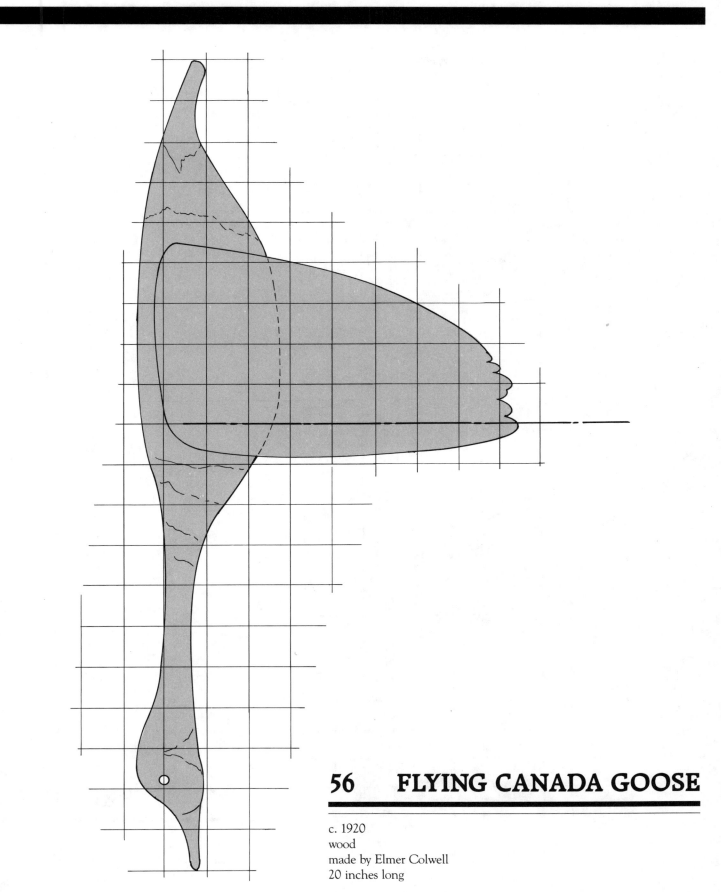

56   FLYING CANADA GOOSE

c. 1920
wood
made by Elmer Colwell
20 inches long

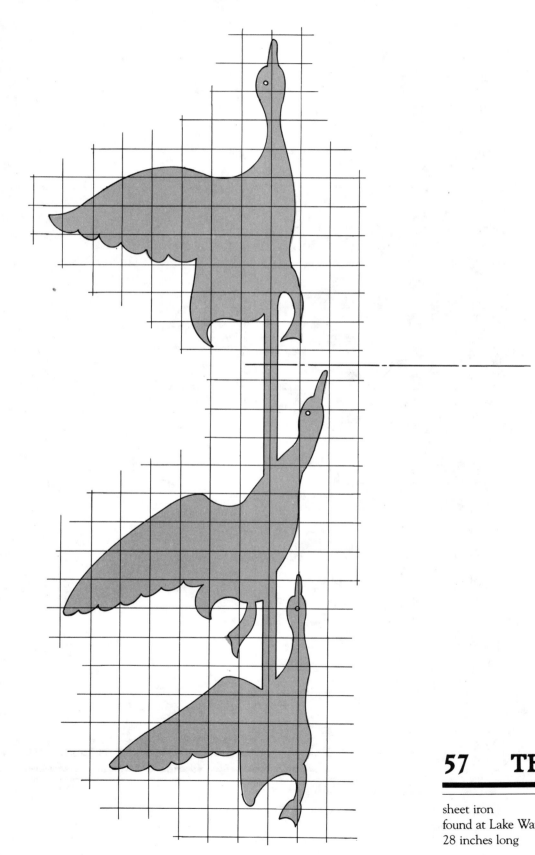

57 THREE GEESE

sheet iron
found at Lake Waramaug, Connecticut
28 inches long

58 PEACOCK

c. 1800
wrought iron
found in Pennsylvania
35 inches long

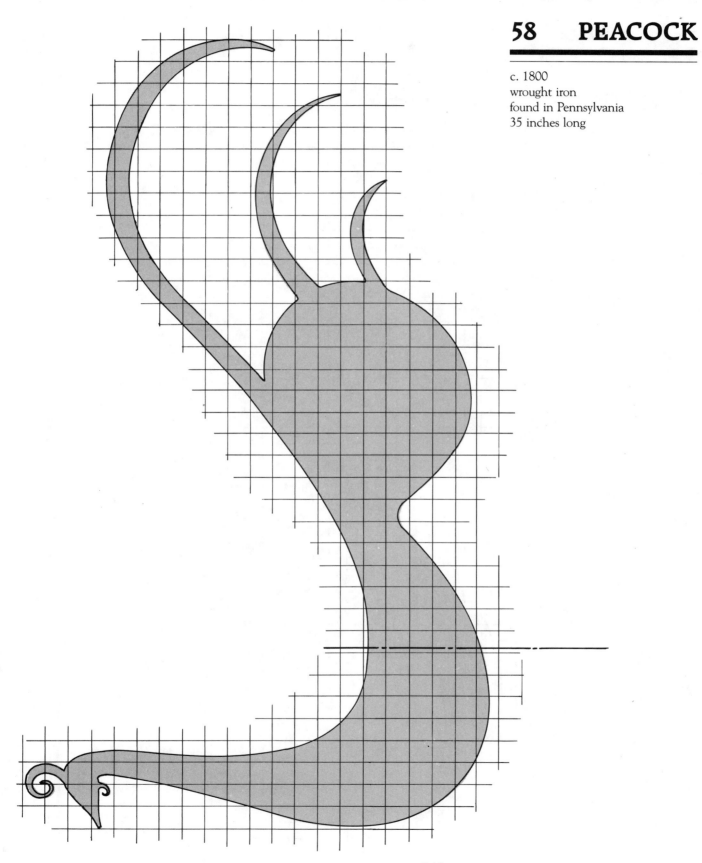

59   SWAN

c. 1845
found in Weare, New Hampshire
48½ inches wide

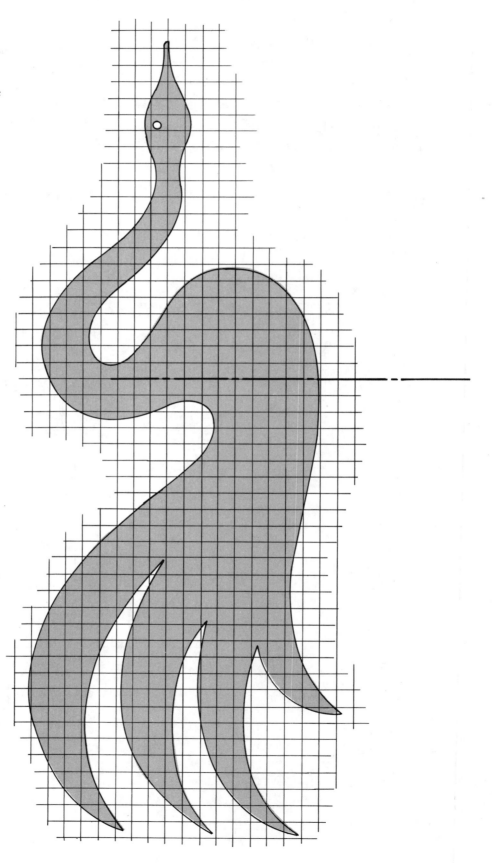

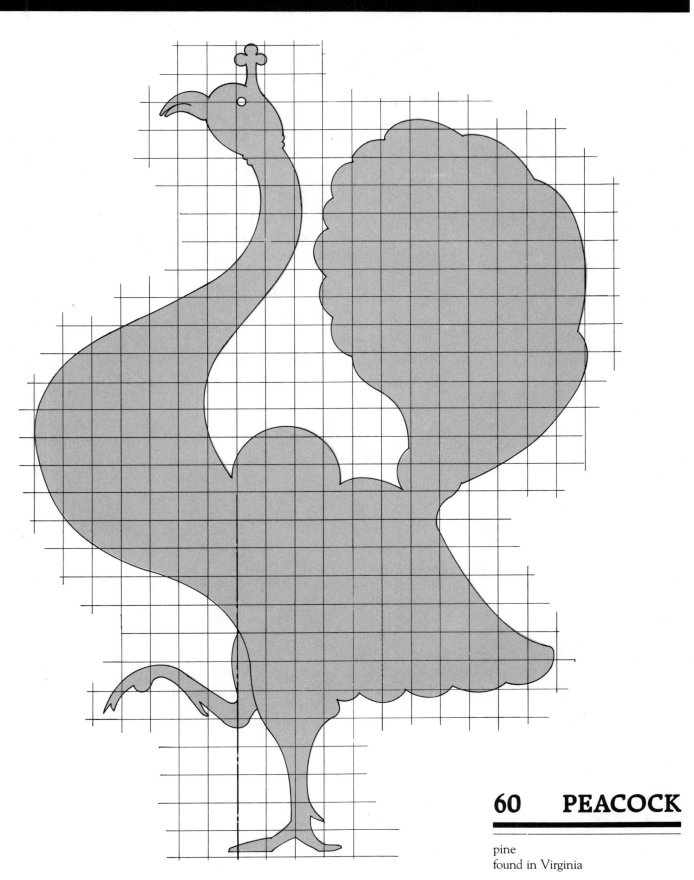

60 PEACOCK

pine
found in Virginia

SHIPS

Ship weather vanes were an obvious choice for the settlers who lived along the Atlantic seacoast of America. Sailing vessels, especially, offered excellent weather vane designs, since the ships themselves moved under wind power. Fully rigged ship weather vanes, the most popular of all nautical motifs, move in the wind so naturally that they appear to be sailing on the sea. Most early ship weather vanes, however, were produced by unskilled craftsmen and were very crude. Because these early weather vanes were fashioned from wood, very few originals survived the rigors of maritime weather.

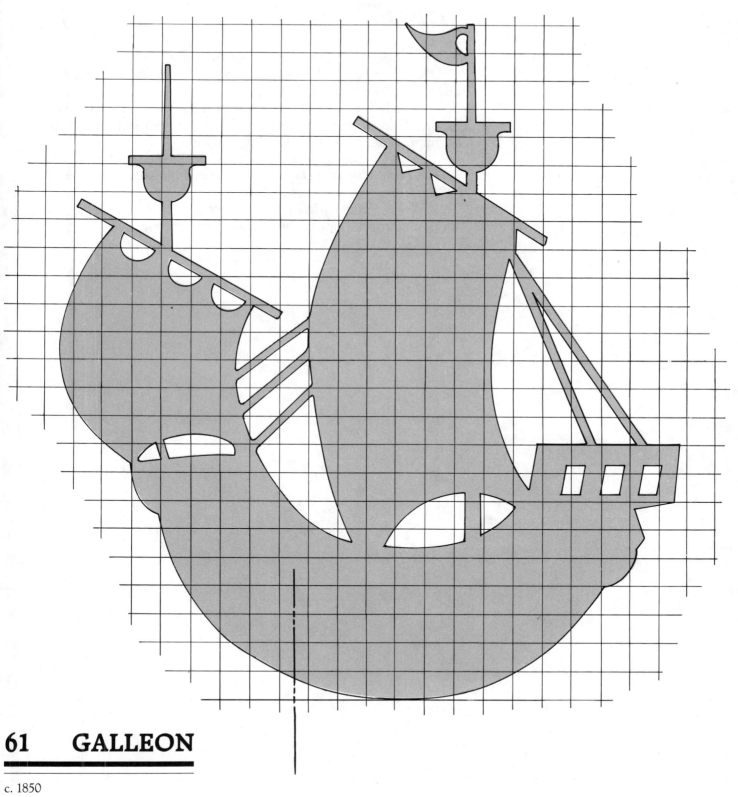

61   GALLEON

c. 1850
sheet metal

TRAINS

With the expansion of the United States in the 1860s and 1870s, and with the joining of the Union Pacific and Central Pacific railroads in 1869, the train became a very important part of everyday life. Until the end of World War I, the train was the primary means of travel in this country. Railroad stations were being built in every town and nearly all had train weather vanes mounted on their roofs.

Many locomotive weather vanes were three-dimensional. These weather vanes were very elaborate and were themselves mechanical wonders.

Silhouettes of early engines and tenders have become popular motifs, and originals are highly prized by train buffs.

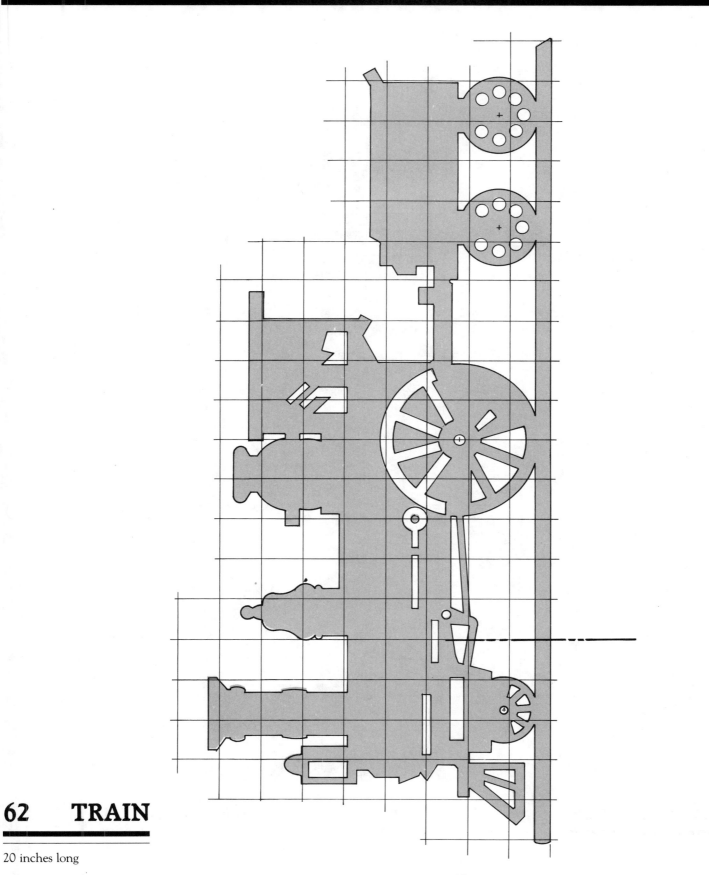

62   TRAIN

20 inches long

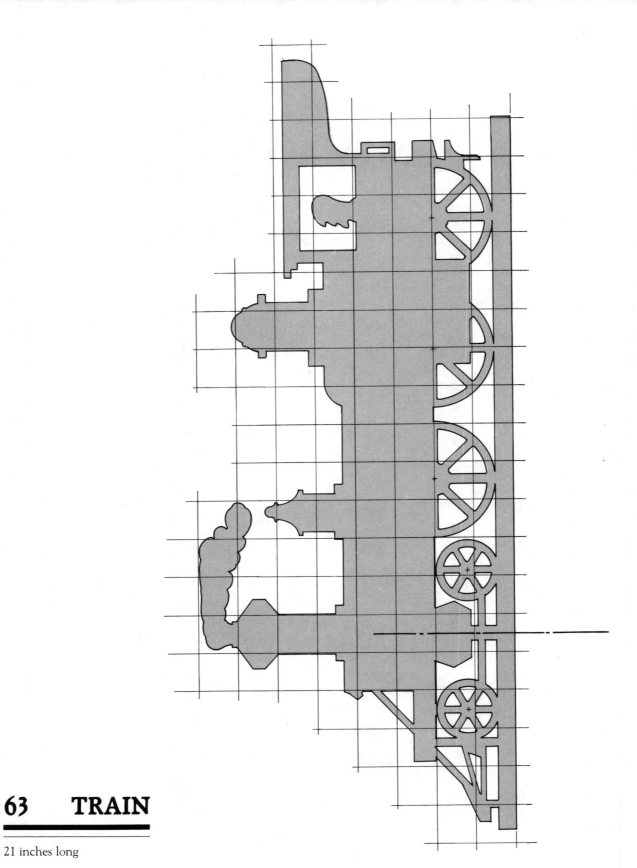

63　TRAIN

21 inches long

ARROWS AND BANNERS

Arrows were probably the first weather vanes. They are very functional and simple in design. Almost all weather vanes use an arrow somewhere to literally point out the direction from which the wind is blowing.

Banners were used as weather vane motifs as far back as the days of knights and nobles. They were displayed on the highest points of castles. Originals from the fourteenth and fifteenth centuries are still found atop some buildings and in museums of England and Europe.

Most banners made in early America were fashioned to resemble those in England and Europe. Later on, American banners incorporated arrowheads and even arrow tail feathers within their designs—a departure from the weather vanes of the Old World.

Some early banner weather vanes were designed by Benjamin Franklin and Thomas Jefferson in the 1790s. Thomas Jefferson had a unique design for the weather vane at his home in Monticello. Its motif was a banner, but the main shaft projected below the roof into the ceiling of the room below. An indicator on this shaft just below the ceiling turned with the vane on the roof. Consequently, it wasn't necessary to go outside to see which direction the wind was blowing. This arrangement was especially useful at night.

64   BANNER

c. 1800
made by A. B. and W. T. Westervelt
19 inches long

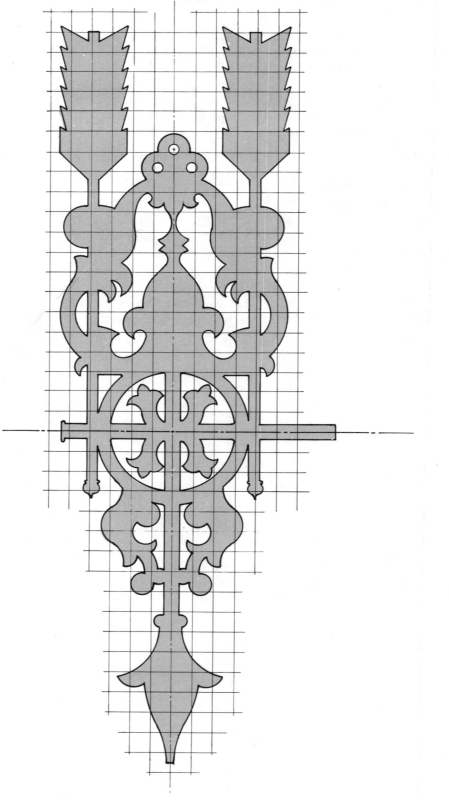

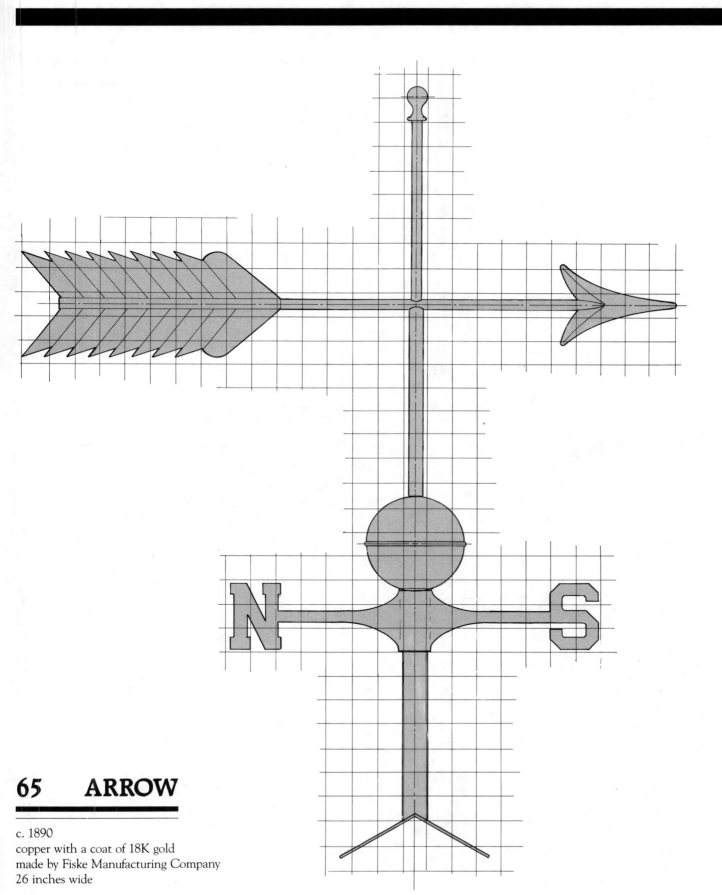

65 ARROW

c. 1890
copper with a coat of 18K gold
made by Fiske Manufacturing Company
26 inches wide

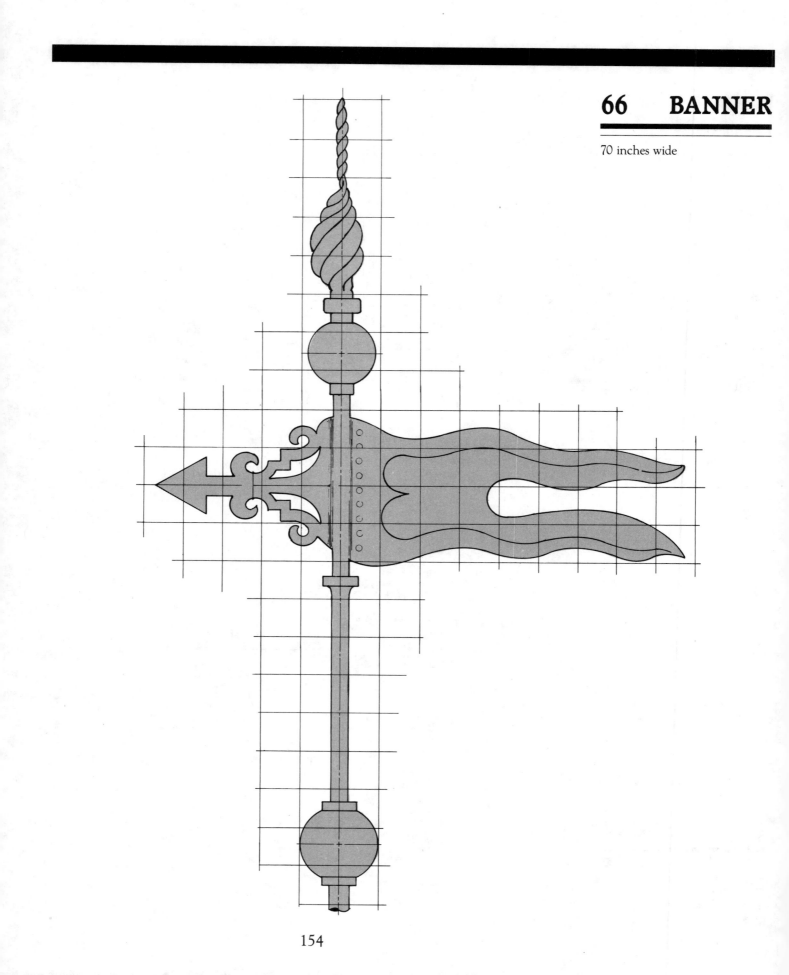

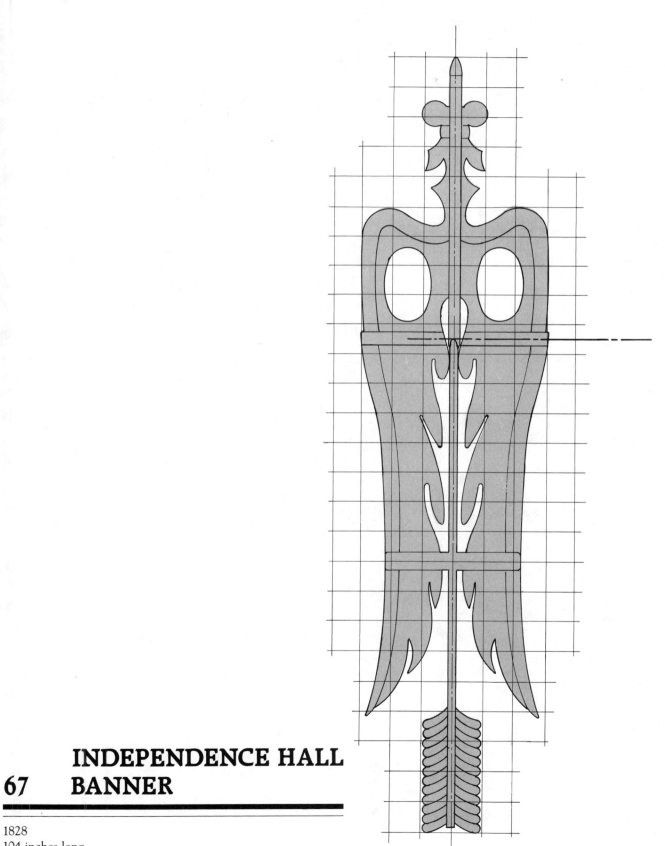

INDEPENDENCE HALL
67 BANNER

1828
104 inches long

INDIANS

Legend has it that an Indian weather vane mounted on a rooftop indicated that the land around the house had been legally purchased from an Indian tribe. Such a weather vane was supposed to indicate that the inhabitants wanted to live in peace with their native neighbors, thereby sparing the house and barn from Indian attack.

The Indian motif was not limited to weather vanes. This design was even used on the front lamp of an early train locomotive.

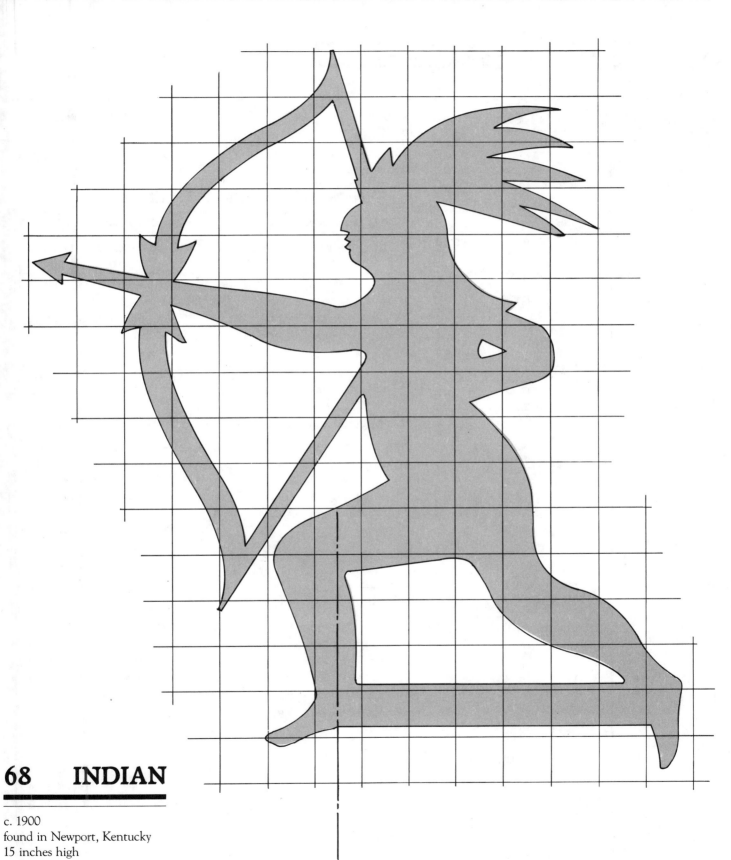

68   INDIAN

c. 1900
found in Newport, Kentucky
15 inches high

Metric Equivalents

INCHES TO MILLIMETRES

IN.	MM	IN.	MM
1	25.4	51	1295.4
2	50.8	52	1320.8
3	76.2	53	1346.2
4	101.6	54	1371.6
5	127.0	55	1397.0
6	152.4	56	1422.4
7	177.8	57	1447.8
8	203.2	58	1473.2
9	228.6	59	1498.6
10	254.0	60	1524.0
11	279.4	61	1549.4
12	304.8	62	1574.8
13	330.2	63	1600.2
14	355.6	64	1625.6
15	381.0	65	1651.0
16	406.4	66	1676.4
17	431.8	67	1701.8
18	457.2	68	1727.2
19	482.6	69	1752.6
20	508.0	70	1778.0
21	533.4	71	1803.4
22	558.8	72	1828.8
23	584.2	73	1854.2
24	609.6	74	1879.6
25	635.0	75	1905.0
26	660.4	76	1930.4
27	685.8	77	1955.8
28	711.2	78	1981.2
29	736.6	79	2006.6
30	762.0	80	2032.0
31	787.4	81	2057.4
32	812.8	82	2082.8
33	838.2	83	2108.2
34	863.6	84	2133.6
35	889.0	85	2159.0
36	914.4	86	2184.4
37	939.8	87	2209.8
38	965.2	88	2235.2
39	990.6	89	2260.6
40	1016.0	90	2286.0
41	1041.4	91	2311.4
42	1066.8	92	2336.8
43	1092.2	93	2362.2
44	1117.6	94	2387.6
45	1143.0	95	2413.0
46	1168.4	96	2438.4
47	1193.8	97	2463.8
48	1219.2	98	2489.2
49	1244.6	99	2514.6
50	1270.0	100	2540.0

The above table is exact on the basis: 1 in. = 25.4 mm

U.S. TO METRIC

1 inch = 2.540 centimetres
1 foot = .305 metre
1 yard = .914 metre
1 mile = 1.609 kilometres

METRIC TO U.S.

1 millimetre = .039 inch
1 centimetre = .394 inch
1 metre = 3.281 feet or 1.094 yards
1 kilometre = .621 mile

INCH-METRIC EQUIVALENTS

FRACTION	DECIMAL EQUIVALENT CUSTOMARY (IN.)	DECIMAL EQUIVALENT METRIC (MM)	FRACTION	DECIMAL EQUIVALENT CUSTOMARY (IN.)	DECIMAL EQUIVALENT METRIC (MM)
1/64	.015	0.3969	33/64	.515	13.0969
1/32	.031	0.7938	17/32	.531	13.4938
3/64	.046	1.1906	35/64	.546	13.8906
1/16	.062	1.5875	9/16	.562	14.2875
5/64	.078	1.9844	37/64	.578	14.6844
3/32	.093	2.3813	19/32	.593	15.0813
7/64	.109	2.7781	39/64	.609	15.4781
1/8	.125	3.1750	5/8	.625	15.8750
9/64	.140	3.5719	41/64	.640	16.2719
5/32	.156	3.9688	21/32	.656	16.6688
11/64	.171	4.3656	43/64	.671	17.0656
3/16	.187	4.7625	11/16	.687	17.4625
13/64	.203	5.1594	45/64	.703	17.8594
7/32	.218	5.5563	23/32	.718	18.2563
15/64	.234	5.9531	47/64	.734	18.6531
1/4	.250	6.3500	3/4	.750	19.0500
17/64	.265	6.7469	49/64	.765	19.4469
9/32	.281	7.1438	25/32	.781	19.8438
19/64	.296	7.5406	51/64	.796	20.2406
5/16	.312	7.9375	13/16	.812	20.6375
21/64	.328	8.3384	53/64	.828	21.0344
11/32	.343	8.7313	27/32	.843	21.4313
23/64	.359	9.1281	55/64	.859	21.8281
3/8	.375	9.5250	7/8	.875	22.2250
25/64	.390	9.9219	57/64	.890	22.6219
13/32	.406	10.3188	29/32	.906	23.0188
27/64	.421	10.7156	59/64	.921	23.4156
7/16	.437	11.1125	15/16	.937	23.8125
29/64	.453	11.5094	61/64	.953	24.2094
15/32	.468	11.9063	31/32	.968	24.6063
31/64	.484	12.3031	63/64	.984	25.0031
1/2	.500	12.7000	1	1.000	25.4000

Appendices

SUPPLIERS

Fasteners and other pieces of hardware are often very visible in your projects, so high-quality hardware is well worth the extra expense. Listed here are vendors that sell authentic, high-quality hardware.

PAINT

Cohassett Colonials
Cohassett, MA 02025

Stulb Paint and Chemical Co., Inc.
P.O. Box 297
Norristown, PA 19404

STAINS, TUNG OIL

Cohassett Colonials
Cohassett, MA 02025

Deft, Inc.
17451 Von Darman Ave.
Irvine, CA 92713

Formby's, Inc.
825 Crossover Lane, Suite 240
Memphis, TN 38117

Stulb Paint and Chemical Co., Inc.
P.O. Box 297
Norristown, PA 19404

Watco-Dennis Corp.
Michigan Ave. & 22nd St.
Santa Monica, CA 90404

OLD-FASHIONED NAILS, BRASS SCREWS

Equality Screw Co., Inc.
P.O. Box 1296
El Cajon, CA 92002

Horton Brasses
P.O. Box 95
Nooks Hill Rd.
Cromwell, CT 06416

Tremont Nail Co.
21 Elm St.
P.O. Box 111
Wareham, MA 02571

BRASS

Anglo-American Brass Co.
4146 Mitzi Drive
P.O. Box 9792
San Jose, CA 95157

Ball and Ball
463 W. Lincoln Hwy.
Exton, PA 19341

The Brass Tree
308 N. Main St.
Charles, MO 63301

Garrett Wade Co., Inc.
161 Avenue of the Americas
New York, NY 10013

Heirloom Antiques Brass Co.
P.O. Box 146
Dundass, MN 55019

Horton Brasses
P.O. Box 95
Nooks Hill Rd.
Cromwell, CT 06416

Imported European Hardware
4295 S. Arville
Las Vegas, NV 89103

19th Century Hardware Supply Co.
P.O. Box 599
Rough and Ready, CA 95975

Paxton Hardware Ltd.
7818 Bradshaw Rd.
Upper Falls, MD 21156

The Renovators' Supply
Millers Falls, MA 01349

The Shop, Inc.
R.D. 1, Box 207A
Oley, PA 19547

Ritter and Son Hardware
Gualala, CA 95445

VENEERING

Croffwood Mills
R.D. 1, Box 14
Driftwood, PA 15832

Bob Morgan Woodworking Supplies
1123 Bardstown Rd.
Louisville, KY 40204

GENERAL CATALOGS

Brookstone Co.
Vose Farm Rd.
Peterborough, NH 03458

Constantine
2050 Eastchester Rd.
Bronx, NY 10461

Cryder Creek Wood Shoppe, Inc.
P.O. Box 19
Whitesville, NY 14897

Cherry Tree Toys, Inc.
P.O. Box 369
Belmont, OH 43718

The Fine Tool Shops
20 Backus Ave.
P.O. Box 1262
Danbury, CT 06810

Klockit (clock movements)
P.O. Box 636
Lake Geneva, WI 53147

Leichtung, Inc.
4944 Commerce Pkwy.
Cleveland, OH 44128

Meisel Hardware Specialties
P.O. Box 70
Mound, MN 55364

Silvo Hardware Co.
2205 Richmond St.
Philadelphia, PA 19125

Trendlines
375 Beacham St.
Chelsea, MA 02150

Woodcraft Supply
41 Atlantic Ave.
P.O. Box 4000
Woburn, MA 01888

•The Woodworkers Store
21801 Industrial Blvd.
Rogers, MN 55374

Woodworker's Supply of New Mexico
5604 Alameda, N.E.
Albuquerque, NM 87113

WOODWORKING MAGAZINES

American Woodworker
33 East Minor St.
Emmaus, PA 18098

Fine Woodworking
63 South Main St.
P.O. Box 5506
Newtown, CT 06470

International Woodworking
P.O. Box 706
Plymouth, NH 03264

Popular Woodworking
1300 Galaxy Way
Concord, CA 94520

Today's Woodworker
P.O. Box 44
Rogers, MN 55374

Wood
Locust at 17th
Des Moines, IA 50336

Woodsmith
2200 Grand Ave.
Des Moines, IA 50312

Woodwork
P.O. Box 1529
Ross, CA 94957

Woodworker's Journal
P.O. Box 1629
New Milford, CT 06776

Workbench Magazine
4251 Pennsylvania Ave.
Kansas City, MO 64111